TODAY'S WOMAN

At 4:45 a.m. the alarm clock will ring. But seconds before, Barbara Walters snaps awake and shuts it off. She can't stand to hear the damn thing ring. The first thought that flows through her head is a motto passed on to her by Abigail McCarthy, former wife of the Minnesota senator—"I am the way I am; I look the way I look; I am my age." Then, in the pre-dawn darkness, the forty-four-year-old NBC-TV star, who earns nearly $400,000 a year for co-hosting the *Today* show and moderating *Not For Women Only*, struggles out of bed.

Our free catalogue is available upon request. Any Leisure Books title not in your local bookstore can be purchased through the mail. Simply send 25¢ plus the retail price of the books to Nordon Publications, Inc., 185 Madison Avenue, New York, N.Y. 10016.

Any titles currently in print are available in quantity for industry and sales promotion use at reduced rate. Address inquiries to our Promotion Department.

Barbara Walters: Today's Woman

JASON BONDEROFF

LEISURE BOOKS ● NEW YORK CITY

A LEISURE BOOK

Published by
Nordon Publications, Inc.
185 Madison Avenue
New York, N.Y. 10016

Copyright © 1975 by Nordon Publications, Inc.

All rights reserved.

Printed in the United States of America.

CHAPTER I

Early Bird

"I'm going to die before a lot of people because of all the sleep I've lost."
—Barbara Walters, quoted by
Chris Chase in **Life**, 1972.

At 4:45 a.m. the alarm clock will ring. But seconds before, Barbara Walters snaps awake and shuts it off. She can't stand to hear the damn thing ring. The first thought that flows through her head is a motto passed on to her by Abigail McCarthy, former wife of the Minnesota senator—"I am the way I am; I look the way I look; I am my age." Then, in the pre-dawn darkness, the forty-four-year-old NBC-TV star, who earns nearly $400,000 a year for co-hosting the *Today* show and moderating *Not For Women Only*, struggles out of bed.

She slips into clothes carefully laid out the night before—stockings, Pucci underwear, prim, high-collared blouse and skirt long enough to hide her knees when she sits down. Eleven years ago, when she started on the *Today* show, she used to buy her stylish designer outfits retail at Bonwit Teller. She still does. Laying out her clothes the night before, of course, is one of the little tricks that helps make waking up before the milkman bearable. It's also a time-honored tradition in the NBC earlybird corps. When Hugh Downs—who is notoriously color blind—anchored the show during the 1960s, his wife Ruth was on permanent valet call. Every night she would select and color co-ordinate his wardrobe for the next day. The Downses also worked out a numerical system for those times when Ruth was away. Numbers, denoting which garments didn't clash, were sewn into all of Hugh's working clothes, so that he could dress himself in the morning without leaving the house looking like the NBC peacock.

For Barbara, getting ready by the dawn's early light takes barely fifteen minutes. Aside from slipping into her clothes, all she does is dab on a touch of makeup, "so I don't shock the cameramen at that hour of the morning." But, even before her first cup of coffee, Barbara has a lot going for her. Five feet, five inches tall, she is still a trim size eight with no vitamins and next to no dieting. Her dark hair is professionally lightened to bring out the green of her eyes. She has the hands of a pianist or a surgeon—long and tapered, expressive but not fragile. In profile, she has been compared to a young Tallulah Bankhead.

She has beauty, brains, power—one of the most envied jobs in television. Yet, there are flaws in the picture. Her salary is truly fabulous—but the government takes three quarters of it in taxes. And then there's her personal life. Barbara used to be fond of telling magazine interviewers, when describing her pre-dawn wake-up routine, that she dressed in darkness every morning. She didn't turn her bedroom light on because she didn't want to disturb the man who was sleeping next to her—her husband Lee Guber. But she doesn't tell that story anymore. In July 1972, Lee moved out for good.

Old habits are hard to break, however. Barbara still dresses in the dark every morning. And she still sneaks out of her apartment like a prowler on the run, but she tiptoes gingerly for another reason. She doesn't want to wake her five-year-old daughter, Jacqueline.

Downstairs, on Manhattan's West 57th Street where Barbara Walters lives, the city looks eerily deserted at that hour. A few bums are dozing outside Carnegie Hall. A truck loaded down with corn muffins and Danish pulls up at the corner Chock Full of Nuts. All the book stores and record shops that dot the street are shuttered, grilled and gated, double locked and triple locked.

But Barbara comes downstairs and hurries to the curb. An NBC limousine is waiting to chauffeur her to the studio. The eight block ride to Rockefeller Center takes under five minutes and Barbara who, along with the breadbakers and muggers of New York, may be the only human being up at that hour, knows the route by heart. But she still peers out the limousine window with a sharp, protective eye, surveying the street scene, constantly on the look-out for a good story.

Once, at a dinner party, her pre-dawn street knowledge finally came in handy. She was introduced to New York Police Commissioner Patrick Murphy, who was embroiled in a discussion about New Yorkers' famed public apathy. When the commissioner brought up the point that if citizens who witnessed crimes would only report them, it would greatly help the police, Barbara casually mentioned that, while driving past Radio City Music Hall at five a.m., she had seen people being mugged. Couldn't something be done about it? Well—thanks to Barbara's taking the police commissioner at his word—something was. The very next morning the whole Rockefeller Center area was saturated with patrolmen.

Barbara Walters may enjoy her role as early-morning civic watchdog, but she has never relished getting up when the stars are still out. She is a city girl, not a country girl, by background and temperament; and, chances are, if she ever retires from the *Today* show, she'll have no trouble sleeping till noon. What she'd really like to be able to do, she once told an interviewer, is stay up all night reading a trashy novel.

Of course, insane hours—and griping about it—go with the territory; *Today's stars have been moaning about having to be at their best at six a.m. since Dave Garroway hosted the show in the 1950s—and Barbara has certainly filled her share of newsprint on the subject. In 1971, she informed Look* magazine: "I don't like the hours—ever, ever. I'm not adjusted to it— you never adjust, but everyone thinks you do . . . there are days when you are so exhausted, you think there just has to be another life. But nobody forces me to do this. I enjoy it."

A year earlier in her autobiographical advice book, *How to Talk with Practically Anybody about Practically Anything*, Barbara had written: "Sometimes when I wake up at 4:30 a.m., I feel I can't possibly wash my face, brush my teeth, put on clothes and makeup and smile for everybody at

7:00 a.m. But I must, so I do." She revealed that her secret way of forcing herself off her pillow and into her Puccis was to concentrate exclusively on one step at a time, blocking out everything else from her mind. On really bad days, she plays a mental game that never fails; she promises herself that she'll cancel all her appointments and head straight for home as soon as the show is over at 9:00 a.m. But by the time 9:00 a.m. rolls around, she says, she's invariably so wrapped up in her work she's completely lost all her "pre-dawn aches and pains."

When Barbara's car arrives at the NBC building around five she goes directly to the makeup room to get painted, powdered, coiffed and combed. She makes girlish small talk with the hair stylist while leisurely sipping coffee in a styrofoam cup and munching on a bagel. (The coffee is a must, but the Walters breakfast menu changes periodically. Sometimes, she starts off her day with chocolate brownies or Boursin cheese and crackers. Whatever the choice, though, the fare is bound to be sweet, starchy and light on protein. When interviewers catch sight of her morning meal, Barbara confesses—"I know, I know, one day I'm going to come down with pellagra!"—and cheerfully goes right on munching.)

By 6 a.m., one hour before airtime, Barbara is on the set, seated behind the *Today* show desk, while the crew works quietly and efficiently around her setting up lights and adjusting camera angles. Then, Barbara walks over to another part of the set to arrange props for the commercials. It seems incongruous to see the woman who has grilled princes and Presidents on the air, holding up a can of Alpo dog food, but it's all part of her job. Critics find the fact that she slings dog food appalling. They claim it lessens her credibility as a newswoman. But Barbara, winner of an Emmy as best daytime talk host, doesn't agree. She does the commercials, with no reward from the sponsors, because she thinks it's good for her TV image. According to Barbara, it brings her down to earth in the viewers' eyes. It keeps her human—a woman they can easily identify with.

The hour-long lull before airtime is one of the few truly relaxing pockets in Barbara's day. She chats with Jim Hartz, Gene Shalit and producer Stuart Schulberg, maybe writes a letter to a friend or scribbles a shopping list for her maid. Before going on the air, Barbara spends a few minutes talking with guests she'll be interviewing later on the show. It's a warm-up technique that serves a double purpose. If the guest is nervous or ill at ease, it helps him relax; and Barbara can make some quick mental notes as to how to best draw the person out on the air.

And what a collection of subjects come her way! One day Barbara Walters may be treating the ten million viewers of the *Today* show to a complex foreign policy discussion by Henry Kissinger; the next day that same swivel chair may be filled by a Hollywood starlet or the author of a new sex manual.

But whoever (and whatever) the subject of the day, Barbara Walters is TV's uncontested grand inquisitor. As an interviewer, she has become nearly as famous as the living legends she interviews. Part of her on-camera mystique comes from the fact that Barbara Walters is not afraid to ask the unmentionable, to drop a smartly wrapped bombshell into the placid conversation now and then and watch the pieces fly. The answers she sometimes elicits from her celebrated pre-breakfast guests can make headlines. When former First Lady Mamie Eisenhower was on the *Today* show, Barbara asked her—point blank—if the Washington rumor was true that she was an alcoholic. Without taking offense or getting flustered, Mamie quietly labelled the rumor a lie that has haunted her for years. Actually, she is a teetotaler, but a longstanding sinus condition sometimes makes her lose her balance when she walks.

Then, there was the time Barbara asked Ladybird Johnson if she'd care to comment on LBJ's reputed "roving eye." Ladybird wouldn't confirm or deny on the air that the 36th President had been a ladies' man, but she did respond that "Lyndon was a people lover, and that certainly did not exclude half the people in the world—women!"

In 1969, when Barbara was lucky enough to snare Prince Philip into her lair during his visit to the United States, she nearly provoked a national crisis in Britain. During an interview in the Prince's New York hotel suite, Barbara inquired if Queen Elizabeth might ever abdicate in favor of her son, Prince Charles. The Prince replied that it was all in the realm of possibility, and when word got back across the Atlantic, the London newspapers went wild. Eventually, Buckingham Palace had to issue a communique reassuring Britons that the Queen had no intention of stepping down at present.

Journalistically speaking, those are some of Barbara Walters' greatest triumphs, but like any TV personality she's been left with egg on her face a few times, too. She will undoubtedly never forget the time one of her *Today* guests mentioned Albert Schweitzer. Barbara chattily picked up the thread by inquiring just how old the famed humanitarian was now. There was stunned silence. "He's dead," the amazed guest replied. And for once, TV's most talkative talk host was left speechless.

Even worse was the morning, shortly after her separation from Lee Guber occurred, when Barbara found herself facing *Today's* cameras with Burt Reynolds. At the time, Burt's romance with Dinah Shore (a lady seventeen years his senior) was the hottest news in Hollywood, temporarily edging Liz Taylor and Richard Burton off the front pages of the movie magazines. Barbara decided what the hell—when in Rome do as the Romans do!—and asked Reynolds, on camera, to comment on the liaison. "Why don't you marry Dinah Shore?" inquired Barbara in her most kittenish tones to the man who was willing to pose in the nude for *Cosmopolitan Magazine*. But while Reynolds didn't mind baring his flesh in public, he had no intention of baring his private life to Barbara Walters. More than slightly piqued, he snapped back, "Why don't you divorce Lee Guber!"

No doubt—despite her consistent high

ratings and fan letters from Dean Rusk and Golda Meir—Barbara isn't everyone's cup of tea. It's become a New York pastime, in fact, to criticize her interviewing style from all angles. According to militant women's libbers, Barbara's TV image leaves a great deal to be desired. They see her as a token female in a male-dominated medium, a kind of indentured superstar trying hard not to alienate the network she works for, or the housewives she broadcasts to, by coming on too strong. "She's basically an Uncle Tom," says one female critic. "Her hair is never out of place, her clothes are never wrinkled, and as an interviewer she's never *unladylike*. She'd rather be caught dead than forget her manners!"

Yet, how you call the shots depends on where you stand. Women, especially the more liberated variety, view Barbara Walters as saccharine, ineffectual, on a par with *I Love Lucy*. Her male critics, on the other hand, see her as that dread monstrosity of the twentieth century, the overly aggressive career woman. They accuse her of being strident, too hard-hitting, letting good taste go out the window to get a lively show. True, you might argue that discussing Mamie Eisenhower's "drinking problem" or LBJ's "love life" on the air perhaps fall into the category of professional lapses, but you can't deny that Barbara's uppity tongue has earned her at least a few footnotes in history. She was, after all, the woman who got Richard Nixon to talk about his image as "a stuffy man" on TV. And it was during a *Today* show stint with Barbara that Marion Javits, wife of the New York senator, informed America that lots of model politician's wives are really negligent mothers.

Are Barbara Walters' inquisitions too piercing—or not piercing enough? Despite her critics, she has the unqualified admiration of two of television's most respected newscasters, Mike Wallace and Walter Cronkite. Both men think she's a tough, persistent and often enlightening interviewer who, perhaps, suffers in public estimation simply because she is a woman. Cronkite maintains that if a woman is "deferential" to a controversial guest, she's labelled soft and superficial as an interviewer, yet being deferential is a perfectly valid way of eliciting information from a subject. Male newscasters do it all the time.

Barbara Walters may have her detractors, but she also has a vast, loyal following in the heartland of America, where the numbers count. No matter what new competition CBS or ABC dreams up for the breakfast hour, year after year the *Today* show continues to draw the lion's share of the ratings. Obviously, early morning viewers feel right at home with this Sarah Lawrence graduate who, despite a speech-therapy course paid for by NBC, still lisps her r's and w's. *Today*, now in its twenty-second year on the network airwaves, remains NBC's most profitable daytime entry, bringing in an annual ten million dollars in revenue. And Barbara—who has shared the spotlight with a succession of low-keyed, all-American anchorman—seems even more durable than the show. She is, at last report, the highest paid female in television. Her syndicated forum, *Not For Women Only*, is a solid hit; after five years on the bookstands, *How to Talk with Practically Anybody about Practically Anything* is enjoying its eighth printing; as guest host of the *Tonight* show she drew the highest ratings of any Johnny Carson substitute.

And she works harder than just about anyone else in television. At 9:00 a.m. when *Today* signs off the air, Barbara's real working day is just beginning. Back in her book-and-paper strewn office high above Rockefeller Center's famed skating rink, Barbara grabs the telephone, placing calls to snag possible guests for her two shows. Then, she consults with her press agent,

Nancy Love, about upcoming speaking engagements. Next on the agenda is a trip to the cutting room for an intensive round of film editing. Unlike many TV performers who have no knowledge of the technical side of broadcasting, Barbara worked her way up the ladder as a writer and news producer. She knows more about film editing than some professionals, and insiders believe she may enjoy editing herself more than actually being a star. When it comes to her own work, she can be merciless. She sits in the cutting room perched on a high stool, slashing out whole pages of script as she watches herself on screen. "But when she's finished," says one film editor, "what's left is a beautiful piece of meat with all the fat gone."

Later in the day, Barbara may have to go back on camera to tape a segment of *Not For Women Only* where the discussions—involving Barbara, the audience and a panel of experts—often get hot and heavy. Drugs, abortion, welfare, divorce, open marriage, acupuncture, consumer affairs, God and menopause are all fair game on this lively issues-and-answers show. In one unforgettable broadcast, Barbara stood politely by while a noted sex therapist showed viewers how to prevent premature ejaculation in a male. He pretended the microphone in front of him was a penis—and squeezed it! Barbara later admitted that demonstrating how to pinch penises on the air had made her somewhat nervous.

When her day at NBC finally ends, Barbara snatches what's left of the afternoon for a rendezvous with her daughter Jacqueline (whom she adopted after three miscarriages). Weather permitting, the plan of action is usually a romp in Central Park, sometimes even topped off by a ride in a hansom. Here is where Barbara Walters truly lets go and unwinds. She often says that playing with five-year-old Jacqueline is her most successful form of relaxation. It gives her the same sort of emotional release that some people derive from listening to great music or browsing in antique shops or strolling on deserted beaches. It's ironic. So many mothers have to take an emotional breather by getting away from their children for a while. For Barbara Walters, spending time *with* her child is her way of escaping from pressure and getting back into herself. Blending her two careers—TV stardom and motherhood—is an exacting task, but Barbara (with the help of a full-time French governess) appears to be holding her own.

With time in such short supply, sacrifices continually have to be made. Barbara plows through her daily work schedule with stop-clock precision, so that once her desk is cleared for the day, nothing is allowed to take precedence over her time with Jacqueline. A while ago, for example, Barbara received a cocktail-party invitation from a senator's wife. Without a second thought, she turned it down. She had already promised to spend the afternoon with Jacqueline and two of her little friends.

This deep maternal commitment is a side of Barbara Walters that even her *Today* fans are unaware of. She was hovering on forty when Jacqueline finally came along; by her own admission, "I wasn't exactly the youngest new mother in the history of the world." Quite naturally, she guards that part of her life zealously. Jacqueline attends an exclusive New York private school, where she is registered under a false name. Barbara enjoys no subject more than talking about her child, but no recognizable photographs of Jacqueline are allowed to appear in print. Is Barbara worried that her daughter might become bait for kidnappers? "Well, she's no fool certainly," a friend reports. "She doesn't want to take chances."

Barbara Walters' day begins with her hands folded primly in her lap, chatting on screen with one more Very Important Person, while 218 NBC affiliate stations eavesdrop. It often finishes tumbling down a sliding pond with Jacqueline!

After all that hyper, high-voltage activity from sunrise to sunset, you'd expect TV's brainy breakfast queen would be ready to sack out right after the six o'clock news. But not on your life! Increasingly, as the years go by, evening is her time to shine—especially since the breakup of her marriage. She makes herself conspicuously present on the New York after-dark scene with a host of attractive male admirers—businessmen, writers, TV executives, even a well-known European wine merchant. Socially, she travels in that chic charmed circle that links the world of art and the world of money. A dinner party attended by Barbara Walters might see Truman Capote seated at one end of the table, an IBM heiress at the other—and all the guests might find themselves splashed across the pages of *Women's Wear Daily*, the Bible of the Beautiful People, the morning after.

Barbara Walters likes to go to the theater, visit friends, dine at quaint restaurants. And she's no Cinderella: several New York gossip columnists have caught her dancing well after midnight. It all makes observers wonder just how long she can possibly keep up the pace. As one New York hostess remarked, "I get faint just thinking about her schedule!" Of course, Barbara Walters does have one source of energy that's rarely been publicized. Every afternoon, the moment she comes back to her apartment, before romping with Jacqueline, she curls under the covers for a long nap! Still, there's no way Barbara can possibly catch up on all the deferred rest, and she frequently reiterates: "I know I'm going to die before a lot of people because of all the sleep I've lost." It has the ring of a confirmed mountain climber musing about occupational hazards.

In 1964, when Barbara moved into the vaguely defined post of "female regular" on the *Today* show, she was the thirty-third girl to tackle the job in twelve years. All the others—including Lee Ann Meriwether, Betsy Palmer and Florence Henderson—had either been fired or resigned in disgust. One or two had been let go for actually falling asleep on the air; for, before Barbara came along, all the *Today* girl was required to do was smile a lot, make small talk and read commercials off cue cards. Maureen O'Sullivan, Barbara's immediate predecessor, had reportedly slammed off the set fed up with being "nothing but a bookend"—just someone to pour the tea and pass the banalities around. Then came Barbara's turn.

With her arrival on-camera, a funny thing happened. The *Today* girl finally bit the dust, feather-brain, false eyelashes and all, and television's first authentic female Edward R. Murrow was born. What did Barbara have that her predecessors all lacked? Perhaps the fact that her image was brainy, not beautiful, made the difference. She came on the show not to add glamor, but to be sharp and clever. She wasn't a former beauty queen or movie star or fashion model. She was simply a girl from the NBC boiler room who wrote damn good news stories. And Barbara from the outset was allowed to be something the other *Today* girls had never been—a real reporter. Over the years, her lively video essays have become great moments in *Today's* history. To get her story first-hand, she's done everything from pose as a Playboy bunny to knock on doors in Grosse Pointe, Michigan (checking out anti-Semitic real estate practices). Finally, in February 1972, came her real emergence as a major TV newswoman. She was among a handful of journalists chosen to accompany the Nixons on their historic trip to China.

How did Barbara Walters get to be one of the most successful women of our time? How did she go from script girl to superstar? David Frost once asked Barbara that very question on his syndicated nighttime talk show, and she replied blithely, "I worked very hard for twelve years. And then I slept with the producer."

The Frost show audience guffawed. The host himself gasped. Barbara waited a momentary eternity, then explained, "Ah, David, do you really think if I'd slept with the producer, it would have taken me twelve years?"

This, then, is the story of a girl who didn't sleep with producers and still made it to the top!

CHAPTER II

Yesterday's Child

"I was lonely, skinny and not terribly pretty . . . I didn't know fathers were supposed to come home for supper. . . ."
—Barbara Walters, quoted in **House Beautiful**, October 1970, and **The N.Y. Times Magazine**, September 1972.

Once upon a time New York was a city of bold, brassy night clubs. At celebrated places like El Morocco, the Stork Club and the Copacabana, the music was hot, the show girls were hotter and, according to Broadway columnist Earl Wilson, "the tables were reserved, but the customers weren't!" During the 1940s, when wartime New Yorkers were flushed with money and eager to forget their troubles, these madcap citadels reached their gaudy zenith and the most glittering of them all was the famed Latin Quarter, located on West 48th Street between Seventh Avenue and Broadway.

Times have changed. Today the Latin Quarter is gone—torn down to make room for a shabby pornographic movie house. But while it lasted, that place was really something with its splashy red-carpeted entrance steps, low minimum, good food and lush can-can girls sparkling in elegant pasties. It was a club where acrobats and Apache dancers shared the bill with top-flight cabaret stars like Sophie Tucker and Milton Berle. By 1945, just three years after it opened, the Latin Quarter was richer than Solomon. It was so successful that, when the Office of War Mobilization imposed a midnight curfew on the entertainment world, the club's cash registers still managed to rake in $40-45,000 weekly.

The Latin Quarter had been founded by Lou Walters, a small, slight man who liked to emulate Florenz Ziegfeld, gamble at gin rummy, and read a lot of books. In 1942, when he bought the place from theatrical producer George White, the club was known as a "white elephant." One of New York's oldest night spots, it had lost money for its owners under a variety of names—the Cotton Club, the Palais d'Or, the Palais Royal and the Great White Way. Then Lou Walters, the cafe impresario with the Midas touch, turned it into a paying proposition.

Walters, who already owned two other Latin Quarters in Boston and Miami, often appeared on the premises with his wife, Dena, and two young daughters. One of them—a skinny, precocious little girl named Barbara—particularly liked to hover in the wings, watching new acts audition and rehearse. Through her strong attachment to her father, she got hooked on show business early.

On September 25, 1931—when Barbara Walters was born in Brookline, Massachusetts—life in these United States was very different than it is now. For one thing, television—the very medium where she would one day make her mark—did not exist yet. For another, prices were very low. You could rent an apartment on New York's Park Avenue for $100 a month. Bonwit Teller—the high-fashion department store where Barbara now buys her frocks—was selling the latest chic dresses for $39. And the newsstand price of *The New York Times* was two cents a copy.

But if prices were low, so were economic prospects—and the spirit of the American public. The Great Depression was on. It was only two years since the stock market had crashed. There was unemployment everywhere, the dollar was shaky and, across the Atlantic, the British pound sterling had all but collapsed. The economic outlook was so bad that on September 24, 1931, the day before Barbara's birth, the American Legion convention in Detroit passed a referendum urging President Hoover "to take drastic action in the current economic crisis."

But as frightening as the Depression was, Americans were obsessed by an even more burning issue, the repeal of Prohibition. On the morning of Barbara's birth, the front page of *The New York Times* was devoted to the battle of "wet" versus "dry." The *Times* reported that the same American Legion convention had passed another referendum, calling on Congress to revoke the constitutional ban on liquor. The Legion veterans had joined a growing majority of Americans, including then New York State Governor Franklin D. Roosevelt, who wanted the country to go wet. Still, the battle was far from won. That same issue of the *Times* also recorded the remarks of Dr. Clarence True Wilson, a Methodist "dry leader" from St. Joseph, Missouri, who condemned the American Legion convention, declaring that mobs of staggering drunks had yelled for beer and "disgraced the uniform."

It would take another two years before a constitutional amendment formally repealed Prohibition; meanwhile, those New Yorkers who could afford it were stocking private cupboards and frequenting speakeasys. For "dry" entertainment, of course, there was nothing like the Broadway stage, and in the fall of 1931, New Yorkers had a long list of hits to choose from. At the Empire Theater, Katharine Cornell was starring in *The Barretts of Wimpole Street*; at the New Amsterdam, Fred Astaire and his sister Adele were dancing in *The Band Wagon*; and the Apollo Theater on 42nd Street offered Rudy Vallee, Ethel Merman and Ray Bolger in *George White's Scandals*. On the motion picture scene, this was the year Lionel Barrymore would win his Oscar for *A Free Soul* and Marie Dressler would win hers for *Min and Bill*. The other big pictures were *Cimarron*, with Richard Dix and Irene Dunne; *Skippy*, with Jackie Cooper; and *Morocco*, with Marlene Dietrich.

On the world scene in September 1931 there was some cause for optimism as Indian nationalist leader Mahatma Gandhi toured Britain and drew cheers from Lancashire textile workers. But the League of Nations was in dire straits, grappling futilely with the problem of the Japanese invasion of Manchuria. The United States remained outside the League, but that didn't stop Senator William E. Borah of Idaho from denouncing the Japanese assault as a violation of every international law.

Money woes and militarism, the big problems in 1931, sound strikingly familiar in 1975, what with Vietnam, the oil crisis and current high unemployment rates. But there is one aspect of American behavior that's definitely changed during the last forty-four years—the state of American womanhood. On the day that Barbara Walters was born, *The N.Y. Times* ran a harmless little item, tucked away on page 27, about female chefs infiltrating the Waldorf that now reads as if it had been written about the quaint inhabitants of another planet.

The article, entitled "Women Will Cook in New Waldorf," revealed that the Waldorf-Astoria Hotel was about to become the first major hotel in the world to employ women chefs. The ladies would have complete charge of a special new kitchen that was being installed on the nineteenth floor of the Waldorf. The kitchen would be devoted to preparing a new line of food on the hotel menu—"old-fashioned home-cooked American meals to suit regional tastes." According to Oscar Tschirky, better known as "Oscar of the Waldorf, this kitchen would be for the benefit of those guests who tire of elegant hotel fare and "sometimes prefer cabbage and boiled beef to partridge and pheasant." The reason the Waldorf was breaking with culinary tradition and hiring women to man the Waldorf stoves was because of the general feeling in America that women are the best cooks, especially when it comes to Southern and New England dishes. Oscar announced the new hiring policy while guiding a group of female home-economics writers on a general tour of the Waldorf. He was eager to show them several new improvements taking place on the site, but the ladies—according to the *Times*—were loyal to their pots and pans and told Oscar, "Take us back to the kitchen!"

The feminist movement has certainly made great strides since 1931. Women have won their battle to get into the best kitchens—and eventually to get out of them, too! Of course, prejudice still exists, even in the most enlightened quarters. It took Barbara Walters several years of just being a "regular" on the *Today* show before she was elevated to "co-host" status. And for a long time, Barbara reportedly fumed quietly while NBC brought in Edwin Newman as a replacement whenever *Today* host Frank McGee went on vacation. The network brass held no personal grudge against Barbara—far from it. They considered her one of their best. Still, they were operating on the worn-out, old dictum that a woman alone wouldn't draw ratings on a news show. Valerie Harper and Mary Tyler Moore might monopolize TV comedy, but the news was still a man's world. Even now, Barbara Walters may be an acknowledged superstar, but who are her counterparts on the other two networks? At the moment, they really don't exist. And so far, no network has ever trusted a woman to host a nighttime talk show on a regular basis, although Barbara, Joan Rivers and Virginia Graham have all proven themselves capable stand-ins for Johnny Carson.

Perhaps Barbara Walters has achieved so much recognition, and opened so many doors for herself, because she has tried harder than most women on TV. Certainly, having to try harder was the keynote of her childhood. Barbara grew up in a variety of cities, first Brookline, Massachusetts; then, Miami and New York. She was constantly enrolling in new schools, constantly having to prove herself among new classmates. As a child, she felt rootless, solitary, insecure. Some years ago, long after she was an established television personality, Barbara appeared on a local interview show called *People Games*, back in her hometown of Boston. Host Sonya Hamlin asked Barbara to supply one word to describe her childhood. "Lonely" was the word Barbara instantly chose.

On another occasion, Barbara candidly admitted that being the daughter of a traveling showman had left her with a case of permanent shyness. "I think," she told *House Beautiful* writer Sue Nirenberg in October 1970, "that comes from not having roots in the true sense of the word, the kind of security that comes from being with the same people. I was constantly plunged into new situations and had to prove myself. I was skinny and not terribly pretty."

During the years when Lou Walters was inaugurating his Latin Quarter in Miami, he settled his wife and daughters into a rather Gatsbyish seaside mansion there. Every morning Barbara would be chauffeur-driven to school. On the way, the driver would stop at Lou's club, so that Barbara could hop out and kiss her parents. They'd be closing up the club and getting ready to go home to sleep, while she was getting ready to start her day.

Sometimes Barbara would come to the Latin Quarter at night. She'd do her homework at a ringside table or peek over her father's shoulder while he played cards with cronies like Joseph P. Kennedy, Howard Hughes and Chico Marx. Later, she'd curl up in the light booth and watch the night club show. She was high strung, sensitive, and occasionally a bit of a show-off. Like most youngsters without playmates, she read a lot and day-dreamed even more.

Altogether, Barbara attended five different schools in three different states by the time she was fifteen. In each one, she quickly established herself as a grind, an over-achiever. Not long ago, Barbara's mother told *Newsweek* that in each school her daughter attended "she had to start cold. She'd come home at night and cry." And so, in place of all the party invitations and girlish friendships that never came her way, Barbara sought comfort in high marks and the approval of her teachers.

She loved her father intensely and, according to all reports, was the apple of his eye. Despite his exotic, upside-down working day and the fact that Barbara rarely enjoyed her father's company except on Sundays and holidays, he quickly became her number-one idol. Lou Walters was, is and will probably always be *the* guiding force in her life. In *How to Talk with Practically Anybody about Practically Anything* (which is partially dedicated to her father) Barbara states that some of the most fascinating people she knows are elderly. High on her list of provocative senior citizens are Averell Harriman, Alfred Lunt and Lynn Fontanne. Then, she adds her father who, in his seventies, she maintains, seems to view the world with a more youthful outlook than many persons in their forties. She says, admiringly, that he perenially reacts to people and events with good will and humor. Obviously, for Barbara Walters, the paternal glow has never faded.

Barbara had a rather morbid childhood theory that God afflicts at least one member of every family. Sadly, she had good reason for believing this. Her own family was afflicted on several counts. There were constant financial problems. Despite the fact that her father traveled in colorful circles and was a producer par excellence, there were often no funds to meet the caviar bills or pay the chauffeur. Lou Walters, the master showman—Barbara later publicly stated that he suffered from "the Mike Todd syndrome"—lost fortunes as nimbly as he made them. And there was other family clouds. Barbara had an older brother who died. Her older sister, Jacqueline, suffered from mental retardation. Jacqueline's case was mild enough so that she could remain at home; still it hindered any sense of sisterly closeness and created a certain amount of hardship and conflict for the rest of the family.

Barbara's reaction to Jacqueline was a fierce mixture of love and resentment. By the time both girls were teenagers, Barbara had broken out of her shell somewhat and was cultivating a circle of friends. Dates with boys were beginning to come her way, too. Yet there was frail, lonely Jacqueline always in the background—desperately longing to be included in Barbara's social life. Her sister would ask Barbara to fix her up with boys. The mere suggestion would make Barbara visibly uncomfortable. Was she her sister's keeper? It would take her many years to find the answer to that one.

Today, Barbara admits that she didn't really come to grips with her relationship with her sister until just a few years ago. True, Barbara always did extensive fundraising and volunteer work for retarded children, and she once served as honorary chairman of the National Association for Help to Retarded Children. Yet, she didn't face her own feelings head on until Muriel Humphrey, wife of the former Vice President, was a guest on the *Today* show. The Humphreys have a retarded granddaughter, a fact which they have never hesitated to mention publicly. They talk about her proudly, lovingly, and by their attitude alone have probably done more to help retarded children than all the telethons in the world. In the course of Barbara's interview with Mrs. Humphrey, the subject of Vicky, their granddaughter, naturally came up. In response to Barbara's inquiry about the child, Mrs. Humphrey replied that Vicky was, indeed, doing very well. She could swim, was learning to read, and had a future full of hope ahead of her.

Barbara truly admired Muriel Humphrey's

easy candor in the situation. For many years, Barbara had been unable to cope with her sister's condition and always sought to avoid the subject in public. If strangers asked her if she were an only child, she would reply matter-of-factly that she had a sister who lived with her parents, and then dropped the topic as quickly as possible.

Eventually, thanks to Mrs. Humphrey's example, the day came when Barbara publicly acknowledged her sister Jacqueline by referring to her on the *Today* show, during a segment devoted to mental retardation. She mentioned that Jacqueline now works as a teacher of the mentally retarded herself, and Jacqueline, who happened to catch the program, was thrilled.

Growing up in a home where there is sadness, tension and a perpetual sense of rootlessness can have a marked effect on a child. Sometimes, it destroys a budding soul; occasionally, it breeds genius. Tennessee Williams, tortured by family tragedy, most especially by his sister's lobotomy, poured out his grief and anger into *The Glass Menagerie*. Eleanor Roosevelt, left motherless at an early age, then rejected by an alcoholic father, blossomed into a world humanitarian. The cases of distorted childhoods nourishing ambition and talent are innumerable. Barbara Walters' early struggles seem to have had just such a strengthening effect on her.

All her later determination to succeed was spun from that single thread of childhood loneliness, of consistently being the odd girl out. "I always felt that I was on the outside looking in at a normal family situation," she revealed in the *N.Y. Times Magazine* in 1972. "I didn't know fathers were supposed to come home for supper. . . ." She felt an all-consuming need to be *normal*. She fantasized about living in the suburbs and riding a bicycle to school every day. "Conscientious . . . too introspective . . . not an easy kid" are the words she recurringly uses to describe herself then.

Yet, the solitary quality of her girlhood was not without future benefit for her. In a sense, she was already being prepared for the complex path that lay ahead, for the special kind of stardom that awaited her. The girlhood bookishness, for one thing, left her with a lifelong love of reading, and today she has no trouble wading through up to eighteen new books a week, background research for her TV interviews. And the ingrained aloofness that's been a shield since childhood lends her objectivity and a cool perspective on people—two prime requisites for a top-notch interviewer. Finally, those early years spent amidst card tables and chorus girls have left her with an innate comprehension of show business, the mechanics of it all is in her blood, and it's doubtful if Barbara Walters could ever be truly conned or bullied or brainwashed by anyone in television.

The greatest influence in her life, of course (for good or ill), was her father, Lou Walters. He left an indelible impression. What kind of man was this slick cafe operator who molded the manners and morals of television's most prominent female? Earl Wilson remembers him as a quiet, little gentleman who wore glasses and liked gin rummy. Barbara refers to him as "a rather bookish Englishman—shy and sensitive." He started out as a vaudeville booking agent. During the 1930s, he opened his first Latin Quarter, a gaudy nightclub housed in an abandoned Boston church; then came his even splashier ventures in Miami and New York. He dreamed of being a great showman like Flo Ziegfeld, and even wore the same flamboyant clothes and hats as his idol. He had little respect for money; it went through his hands as soon as he got it. At home, as long as the creditors weren't knocking on the door yet, he made sure his wife and daughters lived to the hilt. Penthouses, rented cars and grand tours of Europe were all part of the Walters family plan.

In the vaudeville and nightclub circuit, Lou Walters was known for his business acumen, his unfailing nose for sniffing out new talent. During the 1940s, he personally launched many young singers and comedians at the Latin Quarter, who later went on to solid careers. But his clubs were more than just a training ground for raw talent. His cabarets had a certain image that was uniquely their own. It was the image of the elegant girly show. Under Lou Walters' direction, the Latin Quarter hired more beautiful show girls than any other night club in New York. It was all part of his drive to emulate Ziegfeld. Lou Walters hoped to make his chorus lines as memorable and legendary as the Ziegfeld Follies girls.

Over the years, Lou had his ups and downs in the business world. In 1958, a personal financial bind forced him to sell his share of ownership in the Latin Quarter outright to his partner, E. M. Loew. Although Lou no longer owned the club, Loew kept him on as manager and producer, a position he held until the Latin Quarter breathed its last breath in 1969. "Even after Lou sold the club," one former employee recalls, "he still had a big expense account and traveled to Europe a lot looking for new talent. It was hard to tell, on the outside looking in, that the club had changed hands. Still, it must have been quite an adjustment for Lou Walters to make—working for Loew I mean—considering that he had founded the Latin Quarter himself!"

There was apparently a very soft side to Lou Walters' nature. "I sensed that underneath the cocky manner and loud clothes," says one former Latin Quarter singer, "that he was really a very timid soul. For instance, Lou once confided to me that he took up smoking because it gave him something to do with his hands at a party. I don't know whether he really enjoyed cigarettes. They were more like a crutch. He tried to convince me to do the same thing."

Although Walters was a somewhat insecure man, he rarely let that part of his personality surface. He hardly ever showed his temper at the club, unless he got really piqued. But he did have a sore point—nobody, but nobody, could tell Lou Walters what to do while he ran the Latin Quarter. Once, he'd gone to Europe and hired a comedian who, as it turned out, didn't light any fires with the audience. His style of humor was just too far out for the hordes of midwestern tourists who filled the place. He was booked for four weeks—two shows a night—and every night, like clockwork, he'd go right into the ground on stage. E. M. Loew was fuming.

Walters, meanwhile, was still in Europe. He came back to New York about two days before this comedian's engagement was up —and the first thing Loew did was corner him backstage. "Lou," he pleaded, "where did you find this fella? He's terrible. He's the worst thing that ever happened to the Latin Quarter—get rid of him!" Well, Lou Walters just turned around and walked over to this comedian and said, "You're doing a marvelous job. How would you like to stay over for another four weeks?" The point was that nobody could tell Lou Walters what to do.

By 1958, when Lou Walters sold his interest in the Latin Quarter, he had fallen on hard times. Over the next few years, his money troubles seemed to get worse. On December 6, 1966—two years after Barbara became a regular on the *Today* show—an article appeared in the back pages of the *N.Y. Times* announcing that "Lou Walters Is Bankrupt." The item stated that Barbara's father had filed a voluntary bankruptcy petition in New York's Southern District Court for debts totaling $164,000. For the moment, Lou still had his job managing the Latin Quarter, but within two years the club itself was destined to fall on hard times. The final blow came on December 27, 1968 when the club shut down, forced to turn patrons away because of a chorus girls' strike. The Latin Quarter girls had walked off the job when Loew refused to meet their demands for higher wages and better working conditions. They wanted a $150-a-week minimum salary, and a guarantee that either the third show on Saturday night would be eliminated or the girls would get paid double time for it. The club couldn't function with strike lines drawn; and so the Latin Quarter was forced to refund $30,000 to patrons for cancelled New Year's Eve reservations.

The club stayed dark on New Year's Eve, for the first time in its twenty-nine year history. It was doomed never to reopen. The prolonged walkout by the chorus girls was ruining the club financially, and wrecking its public image as well. Then, shortly after the New Year, a new crisis arose—the Latin Quarter lost its lease and was evicted from its famed home on 48th Street and Broadway. The eviction came about when E. M. Loew refused to pay rent after a bitter disagreement with the club's landlord, Walter J. Salmon of the Atlantic Leasing

Company, Inc. Loew was reportedly unhappy with a clause in his lease allowing Salmon to dispossess the Latin Quarter if he ever wanted to put up a new building on the site. Loew wanted the clause removed and a new five-year lease drawn up in its place. Salmon refused to negotiate—and Loew stopped paying rent.

And so, on February 21, 1969, the end of an era in New York supper-club history came. The Latin Quarter announced it would not reopen for business. At the time, Loew hinted that he might be looking for another home for the club, but such plans never materialized. The Latin Quarter was soon torn down to make way for an X-rated movie parlor. In the midst of the closing, Lou Walters told the *Times*: "In my opinion, it [the LQ] won't open, or if it does, it won't be for a long time." Lou publicly blamed the American Guild of Variety Artists—the chorus girls' union—for helping to bring about the club's demise. He maintained that Penny Singleton, the union's vice-president, had badgered the management with the unreasonable demands for the fourteen chorus girls, show girls and production singers involved in the dispute. In an era of steadily declining nightclub revenues, those demands had proven to be the straw that broke the camel's back.

Actually, it was amazing just how long the Latin Quarter had managed to hang in there. In recent years, it had had to compete not only with television, but with discotheques and New York's quick-sprouting array of singles' bars. The old-fashioned cabarets just couldn't survive the triple onslaught. Sherman Billingsley's Stork Club had already closed up shop in 1965. The newspapers wrote El Morocco's obituary on May 23, 1970—only fifteen months after the demise of the Latin Quarter. Now only the Copacabana, the last of the bigtime cafes, remained.

Following the fade-out of the Latin Quarter, Lou Walters and his wife Dena retired to Florida. Naturally enough, one of the aging impresario's chief pastimes is now watching his famous daughter on television each morning. And as a retired show business producer, he spares no criticism in reviewing Barbara's performances. His chief complaint is that only her profile is visible when she does a *Today* show interview. He is constantly urging her to turn her head away from guests and look directly into the camera when asking questions. Barbara, of course, never listens to him. It happens to be her policy as an interviewer not to take her eyes off her guest for a moment. She feels it helps establish a rapport. By concentrating on Barbara, the guest loses sight of the fact that he's engaged in a recorded conversation that's being photographed from every angle—and in the process Barbara gets a better interview. (In fact, rapport is so important in an interview situation that Barbara always instructs a nervous guest before airtime to disregard the lights, camera and stage manager—just to pay attention to her and kind of let the camera listen in on their conversation.)

Of course, a father is still a father, and Lou Walters continues to grumble about not seeing his daughter full-face often enough on TV. Ten million viewers of the *Today* show think Barbara Walters does perfectly fine on camera, but fathers, Heaven knows, are not that easy to please.

CHAPTER III

Career Girl

"You're a marvelous girl—but stay out of TV!"
—A TV producer's advice to Barbara, in 1957.

While Barbara Walters was a teenager, World War II ended, Harry Truman became President, and a few brave actors in New York were doing something called "live television" on the Dumont network. Barbara absorbed all these events while attending Miami Beach High School and two New York private schools, Fieldston and Birch Wathen. Then, she set off for Sarah Lawrence College in picturesque Bronxville, New York. By the time she was a co-ed, her shell had cracked considerably. Now there were dates, parties, dances, school elections and a battery of girlfriends. At Sarah Lawrence, Barbara, as always, was classified as a "grind," but she also developed a reputation for being witty and extroverted. It one point, she was even President of her dorm.

College was truly the most *normal* period of her life. She longed to be an actress, but was convinced she had no particular talent in that direction. So, she set her sights on teaching, instead.

Barbara attended Sarah Lawrence in the early 1950s—the McCarthy Era—when suspected "Red" sympathizers were being flushed out of every nook and cranny in business and government. During these hysterical years, colleges were not exempt from the attacks of the far right—not even ladylike institutions like Sarah Lawrence. In February 1952, when Barbara was a sophomore at the twenty-four-year-old school for women, its president, Dr. Harold Taylor, became the target of a political witch-hunt. He was beseiged by so many accusatory slings and arrows that he was forced to issue a public statement in his own defense. "Until very recently," Dr. Taylor declared, "Sarah Lawrence College has been spared the kind of attacks on freedom in education which have occurred at many institutions. . . . However, during the past two months we have had such attacks." On February 4, 1952, *Newsweek* reported that Dr. Taylor was spending approximately two thirds of his working hours defending the college against a whole horde or "completely unfounded charges."

Several right-wing newspapers were accusing members of the faculty of subversive affiliations. Ironically enough, Sarah Lawrence was also being singled out by the *Daily Worker*, a Communist Party publication, for its "alleged discrimination against Negro students."

Some of the college's worst critics were banding together right in its own backyard. They called themselves the Americanism Committee of the Westchester County American Legion. This group submitted fourteen questions to the trustees of Sarah Lawrence, regarding the activities of Dr. Taylor and three of his seventy-one faculty members. The Legion alleged that two of the three faculty members in question had attended the Waldorf Peace Conference in 1949, which the Legion claimed was a subversive front. The Legion also registered concern about the possibly anti-American political activities of some of the college's 354 co-eds.

As a result of these charges, the Sarah Lawrence Board of Trustees were forced to respond publicly. They issued a statement reaffirming their support of Dr. Taylor, the entire faculty and the student body. They emphasized that the trustees and president "have confidence in the present faculty," and reiterated the school's longstanding policy of non-political alignment. Their statement read: "It is a principle accepted by the faculty, the president and trustees alike that there is to be no indoctrination of students with a political, philosophical or religious dogma. . . . No person who takes his intellectual orders from an outside authority, whether Communist or any other, could be given or could retain the responsibility of membership in the Sarah Lawrence faculty."

As long as national Red hysteria reigned, however, the American Legion refused to be pacified simply by disclaimers of innocence; and the controversy raged on for two more years. By then, McCarthyism and its impact on the national scene had begun to fade. Barbara, who was graduated from Sarah Lawrence in 1954, had followed the freedom-in-education battle closely—but strictly from the sidelines. Personally, she was all for academic freedom; but her interests were artistic rather than political and she refused to become embroiled in active campus unrest. She may have attended campus demonstrations backing Dr. Taylor, but it's doubtful that she ever walked a picket line or even waved a sign. Already her objectivity as a news observer was asserting itself.

Anyway, her campus years were her watershed of normalcy, and she relished her new role as a middle-class belle too much to risk being labelled a leftist radical. Barbara was so enamoured, at this point in her life, of doing "the right thing" and dreaming the American dream that, shortly after graduation, she even took out a marriage license—and, lo and behold, went through with the ceremony. The groom was a successful young Jewish businessman, whose name Barbara now refuses to divulge. The marriage was annulled after eleven months, and they've never communicated since.

Why did Barbara choose to marry in the first place? Was it love—or just a college fling? Basically, she now believes she turned to this man because of what she thought he could provide—emotionally and materially. It was a very pre-Women's Lib attitude on her part, but then this was 1954. It was all part of her grand middle-class fantasy. She thought she could be happy living a sheltered married life in the suburbs. But somehow she wasn't, and she had to get out.

Even though Barbara found marriage repressive and confining, the breakup hit her hard. She was, after all, a good Jewish girl. One of the Latin Quarter's ex-singers (a man several years her senior) recalls how she stopped him on a Manhattan street corner one day and poured out her heart to him. Her husband had taken flight. There wasn't even a stick of furniture left in their apartment. The man was moved by her plight, yet slightly surprised to be hearing all this. They only knew each other casually. She must have been unbearably anguished to broadcast her troubles this way. It was very unlike Barbara. Even back then, she was not generally known for letting her guard down in public.

Barbara had been working toward a master's degree in education, but following the annulment, she dropped her plans to teach. Instead, she decided to really strike out on her own. She went to secretarial school, learned speedwriting, took a few month's breather in Europe, then landed her first full-time job as a secretary in an advertising agency. From the moment she sat down at a typewriter, however, Barbara knew she was destined for bigger things than transcribing someone else's letters—and she set out to make them happen. Her ambition got her a series of publicity writing assignments for WRCA, WPIX and CBS (where she worked briefly for Walter Cronkite). But women weren't exactly being welcomed with open arms into executive positions in television then, and by the late 1950s Barbara doubted videoland was really the place for her. She dropped out of television for a while to work as a theater publicist.

Ironically, just when her career seemed to be crumbling, the family roof decided to cave in as well. One of her father's lavish nightclub ventures, the breathtaking Cafe de Paris failed—and he went bankrupt. The Walters clan, for so many years between penthouse and poorhouse, were suddenly broke again.

It was the last, sweet days of the Eisenhower Era. Barbara's family was in dire financial straits and she herself was becoming increasingly discontent with her niche as a publicity girl. It wasn't what she really wanted. In retrospect, she bitterly refers to this period of her life as "the dark ages." She often says in magazine interviews that, if she could have anticipated these family setbacks in 1954, she probably would have stayed married. "I would have been too scared to call it off."

Chances are, too, that if Barbara had stuck with that early marriage, she never would have become a TV star. As it is, her struggle to get somewhere in the video business was long, hard and indescribably frustrating. When she first came to television fresh out of college, she went in through the back door and for the next decade that's where she stayed. She was out to make her mark behind-the-scenes because she thought that's where her future lay. She was sure she could never succeed on camera. After all, she was the kind of girl nobody thought could make it. She had a funny Boston accent. Her r's came out sounding like bent w's. She wasn't really leggy or bosomy or beautiful enough to be called glamorous.

Although she couldn't speak with a purr or win beauty pageants, there was one thing she could do well, and that was write. So Barbara Walters set her cap to become a television writer.

Her broadcasting career officially began when she left her ad-agency secretarial desk and joined WRCA-TV (NBC's New York outlet). Her first title was "assistant to the publicity director"—in reality, a glorified gofer—but it was a start, if nothing more, so Barbara made the best of it. Soon, she was chosen to participate in RCA's in-house training program for new TV producers, and it didn't take Barbara long to move out of the publicity department and into producing. She was on her way! During her apprenticeship here, she learned several valuable skills—researching, script-writing, film editing—all of which would come in mighty handy in later years.

Next came a job as "women's program producer" at WPIX, another local New

York station. Then, CBS hired her as a news and public affairs writer. Her specific assignment was to create copy for their morning news show—*Today's* competition—and Barbara wound up writing breakfast dialogue for Dick Van Dyke, Will Rogers Jr. and Anita Colby. In 1957, though she was let go in a budget cutback. Before leaving CBS, she asked producer Don Hewitt what he thought her chances were of ever making it as an on-screen personality. "You're a marvelous girl," he said flatly, "but stay out of TV!" That appraisal, plus Barbara's own doubts about her behind-the-scenes future in television, led her to accept a job outside the medium—as a theatrical publicist for Tex McCrary, Inc. The work was dull, tough and anxiety-producing. Barbara's job was to plant news items in the papers and generally "be aggressive." She hated every minute of it. But, as usual, she did very well at it.

"The Dark Ages" lasted until 1961. That turned out to be Barbara's lucky year in more than one way. On a blind date, she met theatrical producer Lee Guber, her future husband. And she was offered a job by NBC. Dave Garroway, then host of the *Today* show, hired her as a writer and researcher, primarily to devise features geared towards women. Barbara wrote them—very successfully—and other women presented them on the air. Practically from the start, Barbara realized that *she* could be the female regular on the *Today* show, but no one else seemed to share that vision. She was well-liked and respected as a writer, however, and for the time being that had to suffice.

Occasionally, the NBC front office would let Barbara do her own material on the air, but not often. Viewers first got a glimpse of Ms. Walters narrating such features as a case history of a Playboy bunny and twenty-four hours in the life of a nun. Her big break came when she was sent to India and Pakistan to cover First Lady Jacqueline Kennedy's memorable good-will tour. Then came November 22, 1963—the President's assassination. Producer Al Morgan—the man generally credited with launching Barbara Walter's on-screen career—sent her to Washington to cover the bleak mourning period. Morgan later told *The N.Y. Times Magazine* that Barbara was the only woman he could have sent—the only one with the intelligence and maturity that the situation called for. Afterwards, Morgan was so impressed with her handling of the Kennedy funeral assignment that he began toying with the idea of moving her into the show's female-regular spot. God knows, it was up for grabs often enough. But Eliza Doolittle still needed a bit of polish, so NBC sent Barbara off to remedial speech classes to get rid of her lateral lisp once and for all (Boris Karloff had suffered from the same impediment). Then, several months later, her chance of a lifetime finally came. Maureen O'Sullivan—the thirty-second *Today* girl in twelve years—resigned and Al Morgan let Barbara take over on a trial basis. After that, America's TV breakfast hour was never quite the same.

CHAPTER IV

Morning Star

"I might enjoy a job like yours. . . ."
 —Heiress Charlotte Ford to
  working girl Barbara Walters.

Right from the beginning, Barbara Walters was determined to make the job of being *Today's* woman a little bigger—a little more conspicuous—than it was. At first, she stepped slowly. Morning after morning, she sat silently by and watched host Hugh Downs (whom Producer Al Morgan once publicly called "the laziest man in television") let interviews go out the window because Downs didn't probe and prod his guests enough to make them really talk. Finally, one day on camera, Barbara just stepped into the lull and began asking her own questions. This taking-the-bull-by-the-horns approach livened the show considerably, but her tendency to upstage the host didn't sit well with the rest of the industry. It's one of the main reasons Barbara Walters found herself labelled "overbearing" and "abraisive" by male newscasters.

Barbara has never cared much how those

with an ax to grind rate her. Her aim on the *Today* show has always been to make her interviews relevant and memorable—and that she's done. In January 1969, she told Ben Gross of the *Sunday New York News* that her personal yardstick for a good interview was "one that brings out something concerning a guest that he hasn't revealed about himself before." And she has eleven years of juicy on-camera revelations to back it up. One of her favorites is the candid comment she elicited from Henry Kissinger on the air. When she asked the reserved, scholarly diplomat how it suddenly felt to be an international swinger (this was in 1969 when Henry was just emerging as a middle-aged Don Juan), he sheepishly replied, "It's wonderful. Now when I bore people, they think it's their fault."

She once got Truman Capote to reveal to ten million breakfast viewers that "it's my essentially tragic nature that makes me do the frivolous things I do." And film star Oscar Werner was one of the few—no, make that *very few*—people who ever made Barbara Walters lose her own composure on camera. In 1965, shortly after *Ship of Fools*, his first big American movie, opened in New York, Oscar did a one-shot on *Today*. Barbara remarked offhandedly that she'd heard he was difficult to work with. "How do you know?" he retorted. "We've never had an affair!" For once, she was momentarily floored. She blushed, began to stammer and couldn't even get another question out of her mouth. The producer later told her he had considered walking on the set and throwing a pail of cold water over her!

Actually, Werner's little *bon mot* to Barbara was nothing extraordinary—for Werner. This son of a Viennese insurance clerk is well-known in film circles for his outrageous parting—and greeting—shots. A lapsed Catholic, a while after his *Today* show stint, Werner was chosen to play a rebellious priest in M-G-M's *The Shoes of the Fisherman*. When Werner arrived in Rome, where the movie was being shot, he was introduced to a group of Jesuit priests who were serving as on-the-set technical advisors. Without much ado, he inquired, "Have any of you ever slept with a woman?" So much for Oscar Werner.

On a far more poignant level was Barbara's on-screen encounter with the late Judy Garland. Recalling that conversation still gives her a twinge of sadness. Barbara had asked Judy how she thought kids in show business today compared with her generation of child actors. With a slight catch in her throat, Judy replied that "we all started too young in those days." Then, unable to stop herself, she lashed out that her mother was the all-time horrible stage mother—a veritable witch. If Judy had a stomach ache and didn't want to go on stage, her mother used to threaten to wrap her around the bedpost!

Only one celebrity ever evoked on-camera animosity in Barbara Walters. That was Warren Beatty. He was a *Today* guest long before *Bonnie and Clyde* turned him into a box-office superstar, when his reputation for being sulky and recalcitrant with the press was at its peak. Still, Barbara was sure that a little on-the-air charm and tact would loosen him up. She was dead wrong. For several minutes, she fired away with every polite, safe, charming question she could think of. No reaction. Was Mr. Beatty awake, she wondered to herself, or really sleeping with his eyes wide open? In response to her questions, he simply yawned, scratched, slumped in his seat and replied in bored monosyllabic mumbles. So, Barbara tried another tack—she asked every hardhitting, explosive, provocative question she could think of. But Warren couldn't have cared less. The same reaction. Finally, even the unflappable Ms. Walters was flapped. She threw up her hands in desperation and roared into the mike that Warren Beatty was the most impossible interview she had ever conducted. "Let's forget the whole thing," she raged at him, and switched to a commercial.

Dealing with movie stars can sometimes be more grueling than handling touchy world dictators or temperamental diplomats. Barbra Streisand was proving a difficult *Today* subject until Barbara Walters found a common thread—children. She inquired, with genuine interest, how Ms. Streisand was going about choosing a nursery school for her young son, Jason, and the conversation was finally off and running. Even though Streisand has dropped an "a" from her first name and Walters has not, comparing notes on nursery schools gave them an instant breezy rapport on camera.

Sometimes, there are sore spots that have to be handled gingerly. In 1966, when Mike Nichols was making his debut as a film director with *Who's Afraid of Virginia Woolf?*, he was constantly overshadowed by his two stars, Liz Taylor and Richard Burton. Everyone who interviewed Nichols mainly wanted to know what he knew about the Burtons. Barbara Walters suspected that Nichols might be fed up to the gills discussing Liz and Dick, so she prefaced her *Today* show chat with him by declaring that she wasn't the least bit interested in Hollywood's hottest love team. She only wanted to know about Mike Nichols. For her trouble, she walked off with a lively segment revealing much about Mike Nichols. In the course of their very relaxed conversation, he began gossiping about the Burtons all by himself.

Barbara makes it a point not to let her guests rely on scripts or notes. She places great emphasis in making eye-contact with them, knowing from long experience how bored an audience can become with a performer who hides behind the printed page. Of course, convincing a prominent person to face *Today's* cameras "naked," so to speak, isn't always an easy task—especially if the guest happens to be royalty.

In 1966, Princess Grace of Monaco consented to make a rare appearance on American television, and *Today's* camera crew went to Monaco to interview Her Serene Highness. It was, of course, a Barbara Walters assignment. Barbara hoped their conversation would be completely off the cuff, but the Princess—despite her former life as a Hollywood film star—was nervous and uncomfortable at the thought of chatting on TV without the security of prepared remarks. In fact, it may be that her years as an actress had left her feeling unable to cope in a strictly ad lib situation. Still,

Barbara refused to be daunted, and eventually convinced the reluctant princess to come on the show minus a list of well-rehearsed answers. Later, her Highness reportedly told friends that she wasn't really pleased with how the interview turned out —and considering some of the things she revealed, perhaps she had a right not to be. But from Barbara's point of view, it was one of her best encounters.

Ten years before, Grace Kelly, the Philadelphia debutante turned serious actress, had given up movie stardom for the robes of royalty. Barbara wondered—and felt *Today's* viewers did, too—how the Princess was bearing up after all this time. Did she ever regret her decision to leave Hollywood? Was she truly content living in elegant seclusion in one of the world's tiniest kingdoms?

After her meeting with Grace inside the Monacan palace, Barbara reported that the serenity was all real. "It has not been an easy life for her," Barbara wrote in *Ladies Home Journal* later that year, "but there is no remnant of the impression writers have had of her in the past—that she is acting her finest role." Barbara believed the metamorphosis had been total and permanent— that Grace Kelly the movie queen had indeed become Grace Grimaldi the flesh-and-blood monarch. And not an entirely idle one. The Princess was actively involved in social work and busy raising her three royal heirs. Barbara also pointed out that Grace has no illusions about her real worth to Monacans. She was well aware of her value as a national public-relations triumph, and willingly went along. "That's what I get paid for," she frankly admitted on the *Today* show.

In some ways, Barbara's trip to Monaco was a jolting experience. Like most Americans, she had always had a mental image of princesses living in exquisite, shock-proof opulence. But Grace and Rainier seemed to be leading a far different existence. There, right on the palace grounds, were a restaurant and souvenir stand for tourists. Barbara was also struck by the fact that her Serene Highness' sitting room (where the *Today* interview actually took place), far from being a gargantuan marble, replete with Shangri-la trimmings, is the size of a very ordinary room. Barbara asked how many rooms the palace contains. Princess Grace replied candidly (and again, a little myth-shatteringly) that she really didn't know the exact number herself. She had once *read*, however, that there are more than two hundred rooms in the palace. Well, maybe princesses have other things to do besides counting doorknobs.

Barbara asked if Princess Grace had any close friends in Monaco, and her Highness replied in the negative. Monaco is really just a small town, she intimated, and the royal family doesn't do anyone a favor by befriending them. It simply generates jealousy.

Barbara returned to the United States convinced that the real Princess Grace is every bit as cool and aloof as her frosty public image. Only once did Barbara actually see the Princess step down from her pedestal, and then only briefly. It was at a royal-sponsored baseball game, which had been arranged to celebrate American week (the publicity festival that had drawn *Today* to the Mediterranean principality). There, at the game, was the Princess dressed in a T-shirt, denim skirt and bobby socks, charging around the bases, and certainly holding her own even though it was the first time she'd played baseball in twenty years.

Is she happy? According to Barbara Walters, yes and no. During the *Today* interview, her Highness specifically mentioned her children as being a perpetual source of joy in her life, and she emphasized that she has known many happy moments as a monarch. But, she said, she believes that wild, ecstatic happiness is not a permanent state of consciousness—at least not for her. "I have a certain peace of mind," she confided before stepping back into her royal coccoon.

Barbara Walters' toughest bout with royalty came in the autumn of 1969, when Prince Philip of England arrived in the New World. Arranging an interview with him was practically impossible; it took the personal intervention of the President of the United States to lure the Prince onto the *Today* show. And that was only the beginning. By the time the interview was over, both Barbara Walters and Buckingham Palace were in hot water, right up to their respective necks!

Prince Philip's stay in America had been bumpy form start to finish. For one thing, he had to cover a great deal of territory in a rather short amount of time. In three weeks he worked his way across Canada from Ottawa to Vancouver; then wound down into the States whistlestopping through Wyoming, Iowa, Washington, D.C. and New York. Even his flight home to England didn't give him a chance to catch his breath—he went by way of Greenland and the northern ice caps.

When a royal consort travels, spreading international good will is a main part of his job—and that means being on constant public display. During the Canadian part of the trek, Prince Philip stood on innumerable receiving lines and greeted more people than a census taker. He visited schools, universities, military installations, a planetarium and the site of a future World Olympics village. He received an honorary degree from the University of Victoria and lunched with the Canadian Council of Christians and Jews. Then, in the United States more of the same followed—culminating in a stag dinner hosted by President Nixon at which the Prince was guest of honor.

He gave speech after speech, press conference after press conference. It was later estimated that on this Canadian-American good will jaunt the Prince took a total of ninety-three car rides. He went on twenty-five plane flights, adding up to sixty-odd hours in the air.

The Prince has never been noted for his tact or diplomacy. No wonder by the time Barbara Walters met him, on the last morning of his stay in America, his temper had worn slightly thin and his patience was a bit frayed.

Philip had already endured one less than successful date with American TV. A few days before, he had appeared on *Meet the*

Press. When he was questioned about the British royal family's reputed money troubles, Philip had momentarily slipped and indulged his celebrated flair for lively candor. He let fly with three zingers in a row. First, he said that the Queen's household accounts were in the red; then he suggested the current financial pinch might force him to give up the polo. (In 1972, Prince Philip's prediction came true. He did give up polo in favor of a far more blue-collar-type sport—carriage driving. This year the Prince's four-horse team and carriage finished seventh in the British National Carriage Driving Championships. He completed the 17-mile race dressed in working clothes (as befits a carriage driver) and afterwards allowed photographers to snap him drinking beer, which may be a royal first.) Worse yet, the Mountbattens might have to abandon Buckingham Palace, which was getting harder and harder to maintain, and move to less opulent quarters. His remarks generated a flurry of criticism both here and abroad.

Barbara's on-the-air bombshell was short and sweet. Would the Queen ever step down from the throne in favor of her son? Abdication, of course, is a touchy subject, but she didn't broach it without some sense of journalistic precedence. Just a few days before, at a press conference in Ottawa, the Prince had been asked to comment on the future of the British monarchy. Did he feel the throne could survive the coming decades? Was the monarchy becoming increasingly outmoded? Philip had not ducked the issue, but replied firmly: "If at any stage people feel it has no further part to play, then for goodness' sake let's end the thing on amicable terms without having a row about it."

That wasn't the only thing the Prince had said in Canada. He had uttered two spur-of-the-moment goodies there that had threatened to topple the Commonwealth. The first was in Calgary, Alberta. When the Prince arrived, after having made the rounds of several other Canadian cattle towns, and was offered a ceremonial cowboy hat, he burst out with, "Not another one!" Then, in Vancouver, he really put his royal foot into it when he proceeded to formally open the new annex to the Vancouver City Hall. Forgetting the precise title of the new building, he simply muttered, "I declare this thing open—whatever it is!"

In November 1969, while Prince Philip was suddenly busy gaining a reputation for himself as the British answer to our Martha Mitchell, Barbara Walters' repeated requests to interview him were being turned down—regally. Each time she broached the subject with the British Embassy, her invitation for a *Today* show guest shot was firmly, but politely, refused. Prince Philip had already agreed to do one American television show, *Meet the Press*, she was informed, and his time here was too limited to allow him to accept other video offers.

But fate was on Barbara Walters' side. It just so happened that when Philip's party reached Washington, D.C., Barbara was visiting the White House filming a *Today* interview with Tricia Nixon. After the interview, the President dropped in on the ladies to chat for a while. Barbara remarked that she'd read in the papers that Mr. Nixon was hosting an all-male farewell party for the Prince that night. This was a typical case of discrimination against women, she teased the President.

Nixon took the barb in good humor. He replied innocently that no doubt Ms. Walters would have "equal time" when his Royal Highness appeared on her program. But Barbara politely informed him that her invitation for Philip to come on her show had already been turned down. Nixon expressed regret about that. He told Barbara he felt that the *Today* show, with its informal atmosphere, would be perfect for the Prince, who is so well known for his affinity for the informal and casual. Nixon instructed Barbara to put her request into the British Embassy again, and see if she didn't get better results. He promised to plead her case personally at the stage dinner that night.

Later that day, Barbara followed Nixon's advice and rang up the Embassy again, only to get one more high-level brush-off. Prince Philip was scheduled to fly back to England the next morning, she was told, so there was absolutely no way he could fit in another television broadcast.

But the President was on her side—and the day wasn't over. Barbara flew back to New York discouraged, but at one a.m., shortly after arriving home, she was awakened by a phone call from her old friend, the British Embassy. They wanted to know if an interview could still be set up for the next morning. Nixon must have done quite a selling job at that dinner, Barbara thought. The Embassy spokesman informed her that since the Prince would be running late, the interview would have to take place in his suite at the Waldorf Towers, just before he left for the airport.

But the fun was just beginning! When the Prince arrived at the Waldorf Towers the next morning, as pre-arranged, he was obviously on the warpath. Barbara couldn't figure what was wrong. Did he regret having agreed to come on the *Today* show at the last minute? Had he done a little too much celebrating at that White House stag party last night? Had he had a bad sunrise shuttle flight from Washington back to New York? For all Barbara knew, it could have been any one of these reasons—or none of them. Whatever the problem, it looked the Duke of Edinburgh was going to be one helluva guest. He obviously hated being here, and was making no bones about it. During her five years on-camera, Barbara Walters had run into all kinds of nervous and neurotic subjects, but she had never tackled a temperamental prince before. Someday she would probably tell her grandchildren all about it—and laugh. Right now the thought of that didn't help.

She was petrified of what lay ahead; and looking at his Highness, seated like an unwilling schoolboy directly across from her, only intensified her fear. Prince Philip—at 7 a.m. that November morning—was grouchiness personified. He looked pale and wore a clenched expression, which seemed strikingly at odds with his bright sports clothes. As the moments ticked by—like a countdown at Cape Kennedy—Barbara became more and more convinced that, in the clear light of day, the Prince was damn sorry he had ever said yes to this interview. Since he couldn't come right out and say that, he was venting his hostility in other ways. He was criticizing everyone and everything in sight—finding fault with the lights, the cameras, the chair he was sitting in.

They were now only minutes away from airtime. Searching for a talisman to raise the black curtain that hung between them, Barbara tried to make royal small talk. She reminded the Prince that she was rather familiar with the royal family, having gone to Wales the summer before to cover Prince Charles' investiture. If the *Today* shows' ratings were any indication, Americans had certainly enjoyed watching that historical pageant. Philip simply grunted.

Barbara tried another ice-breaker. Was there any topic in particular that his Highness wanted to discuss on the air? None whatsoever was his clipped reply. Where would she go from here?

Somehow, she would have to find the right approach—and quickly—because Barbara Walters and her reluctant prince were now officially on the air. She led off the interview with a piece of information that President Nixon had brought to her attention yesterday. It seems a poll in Great Britain had once revealed that if the Brit-

83

ish ever had to elect a President, Prince Philip would win by a landslide. After mentioning that tidbit, Barbara asked the Prince to comment. It was a poor starting place. The Duke of Edinburgh, it seemed, was in no mood for hypothetical questions that morning. He replied curtly that the question was too iffy to need answering, so he didn't give her one.

Well, they were certainly off to a flying start! Right then and there, Barbara made a mental note to herself—never, ever lead off with a hypothetical question again! But that resolve wouldn't help her now. Having nothing left to lose, she decided to switch gears and move into the realm of personal, everyday affairs. For lack of any other tack to take, she asked the Duke's views on parental permissiveness. Are the royal children pampered? Has the monarchy changed with the times? And does the Prince ever regret his own outspokenness.

Voila! Suddenly the Duke of Edinburgh began to sit up straighter and look Ms. Walters right in the eye. Color returned to his face, his expression became more animated. It was as if the Duke had just awakened—refreshed—from a fitful sleep. Now the interview stepped up in pace and became livelier. In direct response to Ms. Walters' queries, Prince Philip replied that he was opposed to bringing up children too leniently, that the Mountbatten heirs were not allowed to remain idle, that the monarchy—in his opinion—is still very much alive and kicking, and that he'd rather be candid and unpopular than exist on "bromides and platitudes."

Barbara had struck the right chord. The Duke was loosening up on-camera, and now was her chance to ask anything that popped into her head. And she did. She ventured to inquire if Philip ever felt like a second-class citizen in relation to his wife? Was it hard for him, always walking several paces behind the Queen, to remain his own man? He paused and assured her with a warm smile, "Oh, you get used to anything. You'd be surprised."

Then came the question that sent tidal waves rolling across the Atlantic—would Queen Elizabeth ever abdicate in favor of her son? (The prospect that Liz might someday step down from the throne so that Charles could rule while still in his prime has been conjectured for years, though never openly discussed by the royal family.) Still, there was no reason to consider the subject taboo; the Prince had already spoken his mind about the future of the monarchy at that Ottawa press conference. Maybe he had some interesting thoughts about abdication, too.

Yet, considering all the furor that came later, it's interesting to note that the Prince really didn't say anything sensational on the *Today* show. In fact, he was rather negative about the possibility of Charles taking over. He said that any talk of the Queen retiring was just a rumor, nothing more, and that, actually, the disadvantages of his wife's stepping down as sovereign might prove to outweigh the advantages in the long run. To American viewers, this was hardly an earth-shattering revelation. But the British have always been panicky at the slightest hint of a royal changing of the guard. To them, the word "abdication" immediately calls to mind the national crisis that was generated in 1936 when Edward VIII renounced the throne for the woman he loved. Logically, there is no connection at all between Liz's possible retirement and Edward's highly emotional departure. If Liz stepped down, the situation would be far more low-keyed. It would simply be the case of a middle-aged mother passing on the crown to her son, the rightful heir, a few years early.

But the British don't necessarily react logically where news of their Queen is concerned—and just the mere fact that Philip publicly speculated about abdication was enough to incense them. When that night's edition of the *London Evening Press* hit the newsstands, with headlines screaming that the Prince had discussed "Abdication Pros and Cons," a lot of Londoners went wild.

Actually, it just wasn't a very good week for the Duke of Edinburgh publicity-wise. The night he returned to London, he attended the famed Royal Command Variety Performance at the Palladium, just as the "abdication story" was hitting the newsstands. It should have been a rather harmless evening, but somehow it wasn't. The stars at the Palladium were Ginger Rogers, Herb Alpert and Tom Jones. They were all introduced to the Prince after the show and were duly complimented on their performances. It couldn't have been chummier.

But the next day a rumor spread through London that Prince Philip had publicly characterized Tom Jones' singing as being "hideous." It was just what his Highness needed at that point—another publicity blooper! Only this wasn't his fault. The rumor was totally unfounded; still, that didn't stop it from gaining fast and fiery momentum. Londoners, it seems, have even stronger feelings about their rock-music stars being slandered than about their queens abdicating.

Buckingham Palace was inundated with

angry mail. Stodgy suburban matrons cheered the Duke for putting down the Welsh rock minstrel, while seventeen irate schoolgirls from Warwickshire—devoted fans of Mr. Jones—actually signed a letter heaped with invectives against the royal consort.

The Jones business was another royal mess. But from a public relations viewpoint, the controversy did have one benefit. It took Londoners' minds off the Prince's recent zingers about royal finances and the Queen's possible retirement plans. Eventually, despite the fact that the rumor was a red herring, the Prince was forced to make public amends to Tom Jones. At the same time, he received a letter from Barbara Walters, apologizing if she had caused the Prince any embarrassment by bringing up the subject of abdication on her program.

Prince Philip sent Ms. Walters a personal reply. He thanked her for her letter, but told her no apology had really been necessary. "It was very kind of you to write such a nice letter," he wrote. "Please don't worry about it." He hastened to assure her that her on-screen chatter about abdication certainly hadn't put the crown in jeopardy. "The early reports were based on hearsay," said the Prince in his note, "and as soon as people saw and heard the question, they realized there was no sensation." Prince Philip then closed the letter by suggesting that if anyone was to blame in this affair, it was surely the British and American journalists who had taken the Prince's rather innocent remarks on the *Today* show and blown them all out of proportion.

Barbara Walters had just survived her first international incident. And she hardly looked ruffled at all.

CHAPTER V

White House Visitor

"Mr. President, do you mind if I kiss you?"
—Barbara Walters to LBJ.

Barbara Walters will never forget the charming old gentleman from the Deep South who told stories on the *Today* show about his life as a horsebreeder. There is one story he told that is particularly engraved on her memory—like a hot brand! It was an anecdote about a famous horse that the mad had bred, and in the middle of telling it, he casually mentioned on the air that "the nigger gave me the reins."

Barbara froze. Since the interview was being broadcast "live" across the country, there was no way to bleep the remark or rephrase it. It was already a resounding reality in millions of American living rooms. So, Barbara's problem now was how to handle the fact that someone had just said *nigger* right in the middle of the *Today* show. Should she ignore the bigoted remark, challenge the old gentleman on camera, or tactfully switch to a commercial? Moreover, she had all of about two or three seconds to decide.

Barbara's first reaction was to confront her guest, and chastise him right before the viewing audience for his choice of words. Yet, thinking it over quickly, she realized it would probably be futile. The man's racial convictions—bigoted though they may have been—were obviously deep-rooted. She couldn't possibly hope to re-educate him in one brief session on the *Today* show. So she smoothly and politely continued their on-camera banter—just as though the offensive remark had never been uttered. Then, after the old Southern charmer had bowed chivalrously and left the set, Barbara swiftly turned full-face to the camera and apologized to those members of the home audience who had been insulted or outraged by the slur. In all fairness to him, however, she suggested that perhaps he hadn't realized how some epithets affect others.

Keeping a tight rein on bigoted horsebreeders requires one kind of interviewing skill—handling President of the United States is something else again. Once, while Barbara was visiting at the White House to prepare a TV session with Lady Bird Johnson, she received word from Liz Carpenter, the First Lady's press secretary, that her presence was requested in the famed Oval

Office. It seemed that LBJ, a notoriously early riser, was an occasional *Today* fan and simply wanted to meet the show's leading lady. He ushered her gallantly into his office, offered her a glass of Fresca, and she settled onto the red couch reserved for visitors while he sat down in his rocking chair. In conversing with the President, Barbara instantly decided to steer away from politics and stick to personal matters. Since it happened to be the Johnson's thirty-third anniversary, Barbara decided to ask LBJ to what he attributed the success of his marriage. He told her that all the credit really belonged to Lady Bird. She was not only a devoted wife, but a wonderful mother who'd had to raise their daughters virtually alone while he was off campaigning and on frequent congressional trips.

At the end of their pleasant, off-the-record chat, Barbara asked a special favor. Could she kiss the President—because it was his anniversary and because she'd had such a delightful time? He mischievously agreed.

Not long afterwards, Barbara actually lured LBJ into visiting the *Today* show. She considers her 1967 on-screen encounter with him one of her all-time successful interviews; and a photograph of Barbara chatting with the thirty-sixth President on the air hangs on the wall of her seventh-floor Rockefeller Center office, along with other photos of Barbara sharing a microphone with Golda Meir, Ted Kennedy and the Shah of Iran.

One September 25th stands out in her memory. It was her birthday—not her fortieth, but almost—and she had a terrible head cold. Her co-host at that time, the late Frank McGee, had presented Barbara with a cupcake decked with one candle, just before the show began that morning—but even that didn't help to lift her sagging spirits. She slumped through the whole show in a kind of dull, achy, sneeze fog. Right after the show, she ran back to her office to sneeze and drink a mug of tea in peace and be alone. Suddenly, the phone rang. Barbara picked up the receiver and heard a familiar drawl. It was Lyndon Baines Johnson telling her that he'd been lying in bed watching her show with Lady Bird, and remembering it was Barbara's birthday, he decided to call her "because you're such an inspiration to women."

Barbara gasped. She couldn't quite believe that the President of the United States was actually phoning with birthday greetings for her. Her sinuses cleared instantly.

She thanked LBJ for taking time out of

his inordinately busy schedule to call, but told him—very candidly—that she didn't feel like much of an inspiration to women, or anyone or anything else, for that matter, today. LBJ laughed—and launched into a story. He told Barbara about a local Texas politician he once knew who ran for Congress for twenty years in a row—and lost every time. Finally, on his twenty-first time out, he won. When he got to Washington, he held a press conference, and one reporter asked him how, after all those years of defeat, it finally felt to be a winner. "It means," he shot back, "that if I can get elected, any idiot can get elected!"

Apparently, LBJ thought the anecdote was very funny, and he had obviously told it to Barbara to cheer her up; but to this day she wonders if he knew how else that story might be construed. Do the housewives of America—to whom Barbara Walters is supposedly such a shining inspiration—sit at home every morning and think, "Well, if she can be on television, I guess any idiot can!"?

During the 1960s, Barbara Walters got lots of TV mileage out of covering the Johnson family. It was certainly helpful to the show's success—as well as her own—to keep zooming in on America's First Family, but Barbara's performance, where the Johnsons were concerned, wasn't always exactly flawless. In fact, one of the prickliest faux pas of her video career involved the President's younger daughter, Luci Baines. The day Luci married Pat Nugent, all the networks rushed to cover the event—although the bride and groom were determined to keep their ceremony, at least, if not their reception, private. Luci decreed that no reporters or TV cameras would be allowed to set foot in church, so Barbara—who was representing the NBC radio show, *Monitor* —decided to station herself right at the church entrance. There she would be certain to get a good glimpse of the guests coming and going, and maybe even get to throw a little rice at the newlyweds. As the guests began pouring out of the church— signalling that the ceremony was over—Barbara rushed forward to grab whomever she could for an instant interview. Microphone in hand, she lunged toward a particularly impressive looking gentleman, identified herself as Barbara Walters of NBC's *Monitor* program and breathlessly asked, "What did you think of the wedding?" While millions of people listening to *Monitor* waited to find out, he smiled back, "I'm afraid I can't help you. I'm Frank Stanton, president of CBS."

Aside from keeping up with the Johnsons,

Barbara has also snared her share of Kennedys over the years. Ted, Ethel and the late RFK all conversed with her on the air. Moreover, Barbara was the first newscaster to interview Rose Kennedy, the family matriarch, following Robert's assassination in June 1968. When Barbara inquired how Rose managed to keep going and not falter after Robert's death—her second son killed in five years—Rose told her, "I just made up my mind I wasn't going to be vanquished."

As an interviewer, the one quality Barbara consistently projects is *intelligence*, which may explain why celebrities from all points on the spectrum—Rose Kennedy, Spiro Agnew, Coretta King—all rave about her. Yet, in 1964, when NBC first took a chance on Barbara as a marketable breakfast-viewing commodity, they weren't at all sure that an "educated woman" would go over on TV. It didn't take long for Barbara and her brainy image to prove themselves, though. On August 22, 1965, the *Today* show's star Hugh Downs told Hyman Goldberg of *The New York Herald Tribune*: "She's the best thing that's happened to the show since I've been on it."

A good part of Barbara's on-screen success is a direct result of intense behind-the-scenes preparation. Even today the woman who commands one of the highest salaries in show business continues to do her own film editing and write her own scripts. What's more, she works hard—maybe harder than anyone else around—to get elusive guests on her show—and her perseverance invariably pays off. "Acutely aware of the issues and personalities that interest the public," *Current Biography* noted in 1971, "she expends great effort and displays formidable tenacity to obtain her interviews. Reportedly she worked for two years to get Dean Rusk on the show and ended up by scoring a coup when Rusk gave her his first interview after leaving the post of Secretary of State."

Her interview with Ted Kennedy was also a first. Barbara beat all the other newscasters to his door after Chappaquiddick.

Her exclusive on-the-air sessions with high political figures may get Barbara written up in *Time* and *Newsweek*, but her non-political guests sometimes cause her the most trouble. In fact, next to accidentally collaring the president of CBS at Luci Nugent's wedding, Barbara's favorite embarrassing moment occurred during a harmless *Today* chat with Leo G. Carroll, the veteran character actor last seen on *The Man from U.N.C.L.E.* Over the years, Barbara has worked out her own time-signal system for letting her guests know that a station break or commercial is coming up, so they won't get cut off while making a vital point. Her signal is very simple—it's a touch system. When the director cues Barbara that time is running out, she gently touches the guest's knee with her hand or nudges him with her foot. The audience never catches these oblique gestures, and Barbara, of course, always warns her guest before airtime about the signal, so that he won't shriek or giggle—or jump out of his seat—when she makes her on-camera "pass."

The system worked fine for several years —that is, until Leo G. Carroll appeared on the *Today* show. As usual, a few minutes before the cameras started rolling, Barbara explained that she might have to signal him on the air, if they were getting cut off, by a tap on the knee or a nudge of the foot. Well, Mr. Carroll, it seems, got a little rattled when his turn came to be interviewed —and he completely forgot about the pre-arranged signal. So, you can pretty much imagine what happened when Barbara got her cue from the director to wrap up the interview and her hand went for Mr. Carroll's knee.

"Young woman!" he growled on network television, "what is your hand doing crawling up my thigh?"

Barbara was half-shocked, half-convulsed with laughter. She tried to salvage any vestige of formality by trying to explain to the viewers—and her rather dazed looking guest—all about the time signal. Mr. Carroll still didn't seem to comprehend. Fortunately, at that moment the camera mercifully cut to a commercial, while the whole cast and crew fell down laughing.

When time isn't running out, Barbara Walters has an amazing knack for getting people to tell her all sorts of curious things on the air. When Mary Lindsay's husband John was Mayor of New York, Mary confided to *Today* viewers that the worst problem with living in Gracie Mansion was walking on the floors. You couldn't wear high heels or let people dance in the mansion because the rugs were falling apart.

Conductor Leopold Stokowski, interviewed by Barbara when in his eighties, recalled the night his baton broke on stage during a concert and how it changed his life. "I felt free," said the maestro. "I don't conduct with a stick anymore." Marion Javits, wife of the New York senator, on the other hand, revealed the one thing she'd never change about her life—and that's leave New York to settle in Washington. Despite the fact that her husband's work keeps him in the Capitol for months at a stretch, Mrs. Javits has persistently refused to budge from her Manhattan high rise. On the *Today* show, she told Barbara that she considers Washington, D.C. a "culturally bankrupt" city.

And that isn't all that famous people have told Barbara. In those bygone, heady days of power before Watergate, Bob Haldeman—special assistant to President Nixon—told Barbara that senators who dared criticize the Chief Executive were "consciously aiding and abetting the enemies of the United States."

Then, there was Mamie Eisenhower who —after setting the record straight about her alleged drinking problem—wanted to settle another score with the American public. Despite what any other White House occupants may have done, she and Ike took care of all their personal expenses themselves while residing at 1600 Pennsylvania Avenue. They never, on any occasion, let the government foot the bill. "Maybe other Presidents don't do that," she said animatedly, "but it was our way."

And then there was Tricia Nixon Cox who came on the *Today* program to announce that two of her all-time favorite heroes were George Washington (because, as the first President, he had the roughest job—he had to start everything) and Queen Elizabeth II (who sets a terrific example for people in all age brackets).

Those who sit in the famed Walters "hot seat" for a few live or videotaped minutes come away with differing reactions. Some find her style of probing refreshing; others are put off. After finally being lured into her TV lair, Dean Rusk was so captivated by Barbara's treatment of him on the *Today* show that he publicly paid tribute to her great reportorial skill. He said she has a sharp style which in no way interferes with her femininity. Soviet poet Yevgeny Yevtushenko, however, wasn't too impressed either by her style—or her femininity. After paying a 7 a.m. call at the NBC studio, he labelled Barbara Walters "a hyena in syrup."

Outspoken guests, of course—whether they're friends or foes of the interviewer—inevitably make the best video footage. And when it comes to being outspoken, hardly anyone can match Marion Javits. The senator's wife was one of Barbara's earliest *Today* subjects, and since then the two women have become personal friends—even though Barbara once confessed to *Ladies Home Journal* that Mrs. Javits' views on life in Washington are "positively unconstitutional." Actually, that's what makes Mrs.

Javits so interesting. For the wife of the Republican senior senator from New York to detest life on the Potomac, and make no bones about it, is precociously refreshing.

Twice since her husband was originally elected to the Senate in 1957, Marion Javits has moved lock, stock and barrel to Washington and tried to live there—and twice she has turned right around and fled home. Her main gripe about the Capitol is that it doesn't offer the cultural advantages —the chance to mingle with artists and colorful creative types—that is the hallmark of Manhattan social life.

Marion's views on Washington could fill a book—and she's already pronounced most of them right on the *Today* show. She wishes the Kennedy Center for the Performing Arts were located in New York because Washington doesn't have enough creative talent to really utilize it. She thinks congressional wives are generally deader than doornails. Marion has a theory that many politicians marry right after college and don't choose women who are really capable of growing with them intellectually. Over the years, the husbands enter politics, travel, meet stimulating people and become sophisticated. The wives kind of fall by the wayside. On the *Today* show, Marion Javits went on the record as saying that the wives of many elected officials neglect their children. If they choose to live in Washington with their husbands, instead of staying home in their constituencies, they often have to send their children to boarding schools—and rarely see them.

So, for Marion Javits, living in Washington would mean being separated from her children as well as the culturally-oriented people whose company she thrives on. Furthermore, she loathes Washington social life. She doesn't like cocktail parties or diplomatic receptions, or—for that matter—golf, tennis or cards—the three afternoon staples of the Washington wife. In New York, she can pursue the things that turn *her* on—theater, learning languages, attending small dinner parties with the cultural likes of Leonard Bernstein and Truman Capote. It's easy to see why Barbara Walters and Marion Javits could become friends. They are both New Yorkers to the core, both hooked on the overlapping worlds of art and entertainment, both fiercely independent women.

It's harder to picture Barbara Walters and Richard M. Nixon as friends. Yet, while Barbara never became Nixon's golf buddy during his five-and-a-half year White House stint, she did achieve a certain easygoing rapport with him—a rare phenomenon considering Nixon's longrunning and heated antagonism toward the press.

On March 11, 1971, she interviewed him for the *Today* show. The occasion was Pat Nixon's fiftieth birthday, and the President said he wanted to pay tribute to his wife by honoring America's other "first ladies" as well (our country's homemakers). Therefore, the specific subject of Barbara's televised chat with Nixon was supposed to be the Chief Executive's views on women, marriage and family life. Yet, as the conversation progressed and gathered steam, despite all the precautions beforehand, other areas *were* touched on. Nixon, for example, seemed perfectly willing to speak candidly (and somewhat revealingly) about how he sees his public image. Somehow Barbara Walters had the magic touch to draw him out where other newscasters made him see red. In the light of what befell Richard M. Nixon during his next three years in office, it is interesting to recall this historic 1971 interview.

Why did Nixon choose the *Today* show to take to the airwaves? Barbara believes she was the lucky choice for two reasons. First of all, she had a longstanding request for an interview registered with Nixon's press secretary, Ron Ziegler, and Nixon—whom Barbara characterizes as "a man of great loyalty"—thoughtfully remembered that request when the right time came.

Secondly, he was far from oblivious to the kind of ratings that *Today* commands, along with the fact that *Today's* audience contained millions of potential pro-Nixon voters (next year was re-election time).

The Nixon interview was one of the big journalistic coups of her career—maybe the biggest—yet it couldn't have fallen into her lap at a worse possible time, personally speaking. When Ron Ziegler phoned Barbara to set the wheels in motion, Barbara was packed and ready to depart with her husband, Lee Guber, on a two-week vacation in Palm Springs. The trip had to be immediately cancelled. Instead, she unpacked the bathing suits and sun-tan oil, rounded up her blue pencils and typewriter, and the next day flew to Washington. Recalling that cancelled Palm Springs vacation, Barbara said of Lee Guber in the August 1971 issue of *Harper's Bazaar*—"Greater love hath no husband." (Ironically, though, sixteen months afterwards, in July 1972, Lee and Barbara formally separated.)

Today's co-host and the 37th President went on camera together at 8 p.m. (a film of the interview would be aired on the show a few days later). Although Ziegler had originally requested that Barbara's interview not run longer than twenty minutes, it actually lasted forty-two minutes. Barbara personally explained to the President that she needed forty-two minutes to fill out her two-hour program, and he agreed to cooperate, overruling Mr. Ziegler.

Aside from the time limit, there were two other prearranged stipulations. NBC had to agree to air the filmed interview in its entirety. It could not be edited, spliced or in any way tampered with by the network. And Barbara was prohibited from mentioning Vietnam or other weighty matters. It was, she had the impression from Ron Ziegler, supposed to be strictly a bit of televised cotton candy—a nice, chatty, innocuous dialogue about marriage, motherhood, and maybe if she was lucky, the President might even come out in favor of apple pie! But this overprotective desire to sugar-coat everything the President had to say seemed to be strictly press office thinking. Nixon himself appeared relaxed and spontaneous. Once the interview got under way, he was perfectly willing to follow Ms. Walters' lead and tackle issues head on. And while the issues may not have been specifically the war or busing or inflation, Barbara did elicit a few footnotes for history.

The "chat" took place in the Blue Room

of the White House, which is usually reserved for ambassadors and foreign dignitaries. Broadcasting from here seemed at first, to clash with Nixon's avowed purpose to appear relaxed and chatty, but Barbara soon learned that this room was chosen by his television press advisor Mark Goode for a very practical reason. Nixon looked good in blue. Still, he was willing to let his guard down in other ways. When Barbara requested that the President sit side by side with her on a settee, rather than facing each other in prim gilt chairs, he request was granted.

The interview was informality personified —as its planned best. Nixon entered the Blue Room after all the cameras, sound and lighting equipment had been assembled—at exactly five minutes to eight. Before going on the air, he chatted briefly with Barbara in a strictly small-talk fashion. He complimented her on the pair of fashionable hip-high silk boots she was wearing. Later, when the taping was over, Barbara decided to ask the President one final question, just for her own benefit. Why was he frequently so critical of TV news reporting? Nixon smiled, and replied in his most charming manner, that he personally didn't criticize the news media. That, he said jokingly, was the province of Vice President Agnew, and left the room.

During their forty-two minutes on the airwaves, Nixon never appeared rattled or put off by any of Barbara's questions. In fact, he seemed so uncharacteristically frank and open that, not long after they began talking, she decided to throw away her planned questions and just wing it.

Barbara's chat with Nixon began like a well-orchestrated tea party. She mentioned having read somewhere that he had proposed to Pat on their very first date, and that the future First Lady had turned him down flat. That led Barbara to inquire if Nixon thought his life might have developed differently if he hadn't married Pat. What did he think was Pat's special contribution to his success?

Nixon said that Pat, more than anything else, had given him a sense of determination and discipline—qualities that are essential to any man in public life. And Pat personified those same qualities herself. She was willing not only to endure the countless personal sacrifices that go hand in hand with political life, but was strong enough to urge him on even in times of defeat, when he felt like throwing in the towel.

What fault of his was it "toughest for Mrs. Nixon to live with"?

Nixon thought his stubbornness was—his

terrible tenacity when he was working toward an important goal.

Barbara next reminded the President that Pat—for all her cheering him on when the going got rough—once confided in an interview that there were two or three times when she hoped he would drop out of politics. Did Nixon specifically recall those occasions?

He did—and, yes, there were times when Pat might have preferred it if they left public life. The first time was in 1952, when Nixon was running for Vice President and his so-called campaign "slush fund" made the headlines. (The revelation of that fund nearly ended Nixon's career in politics then and there. But his famous TV speech about "Pat's cloth coat and his dog Checkers" swayed public opinion in his favor and kept Eisenhower from dumping him from the Republican national ticket.)

And there were two more times, Nixon related to Barbara Walters, when Pat became disillusioned with politics: in 1960, after he lost the Presidency to John F. Kennedy; and in 1962, when he was defeated in his bid to become Governor of California. And for the next six years, Nixon took his wife's advice and became a total political has-been. Yet, in 1968, when he decided to make a national comeback—

Barbara Walters is the most successful woman in the history of daytime television.

Here Barbara arranges details for an upcoming program. Her ability to work is phenomenal.

Barbara sorts through her correspondence. She is deluged with mail from fans across the country.

Barbara Walters proudly holds her Emmy Award—a fitting tribute to a most capable commentator.

Barbara Walters finds herself hemmed in by the crowds at the premiere of the film of another famous Barbra—Streisand's "Funny Lady."

Barbara Walters receives the coveted award aboard the New York Hudson River Dayliner where the New York Emmy Awards were held this year.

The two stars of the award winning *Today Show*, **Barbara Walters and Jim Hartz.**

Ms. Walters wore this lovely outfit to an NBC Affiliate party in Hollywood in May of 1973.

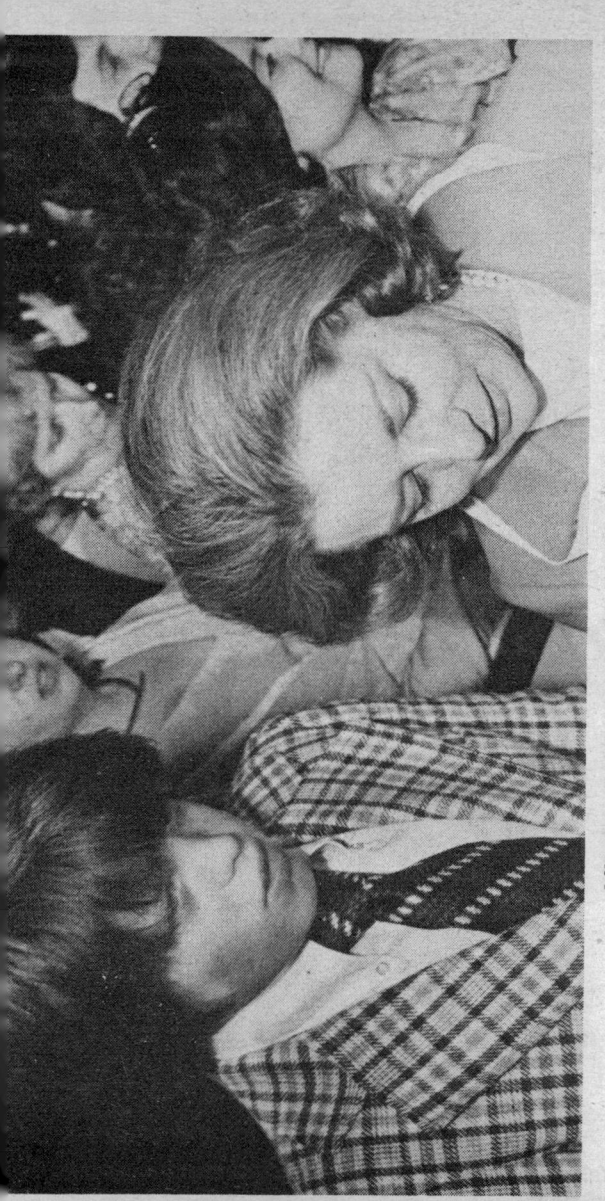

Like most of the celebrities at the opening of "Funny Lady" at the Kennedy Center in Washington, D.C., Barbara Walters was besieged by fans asking for autographs. Here she signs one for a young admirer.

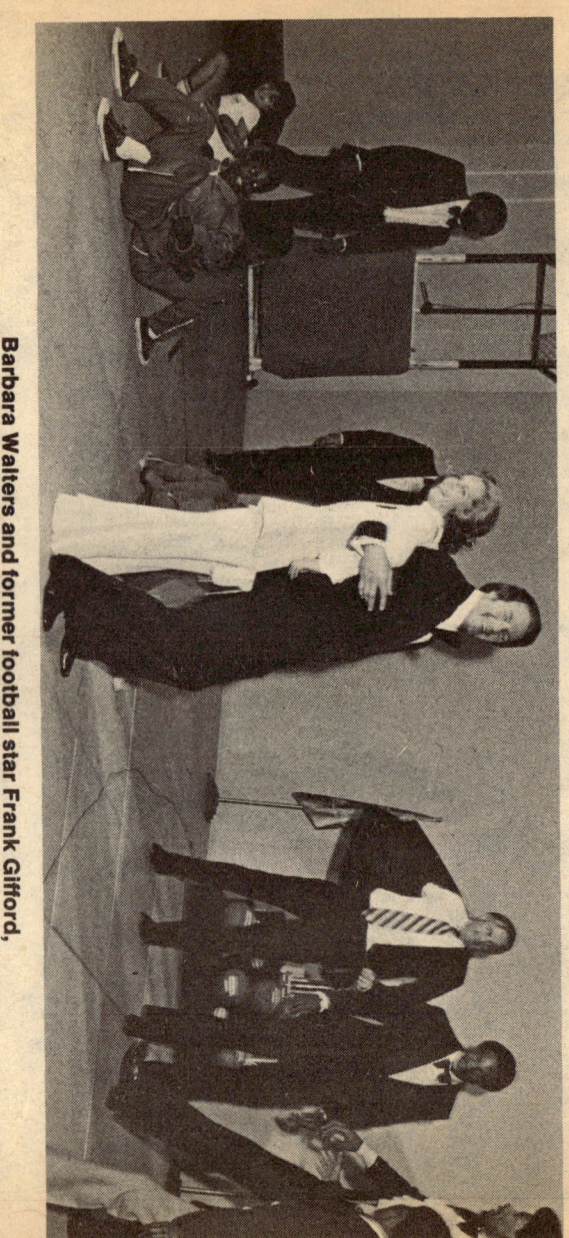

Barbara Walters and former football star Frank Gifford, now a TV sports commentator, try their hand at warm-up exercises as practiced by the Special Olympics for Retarded Children.

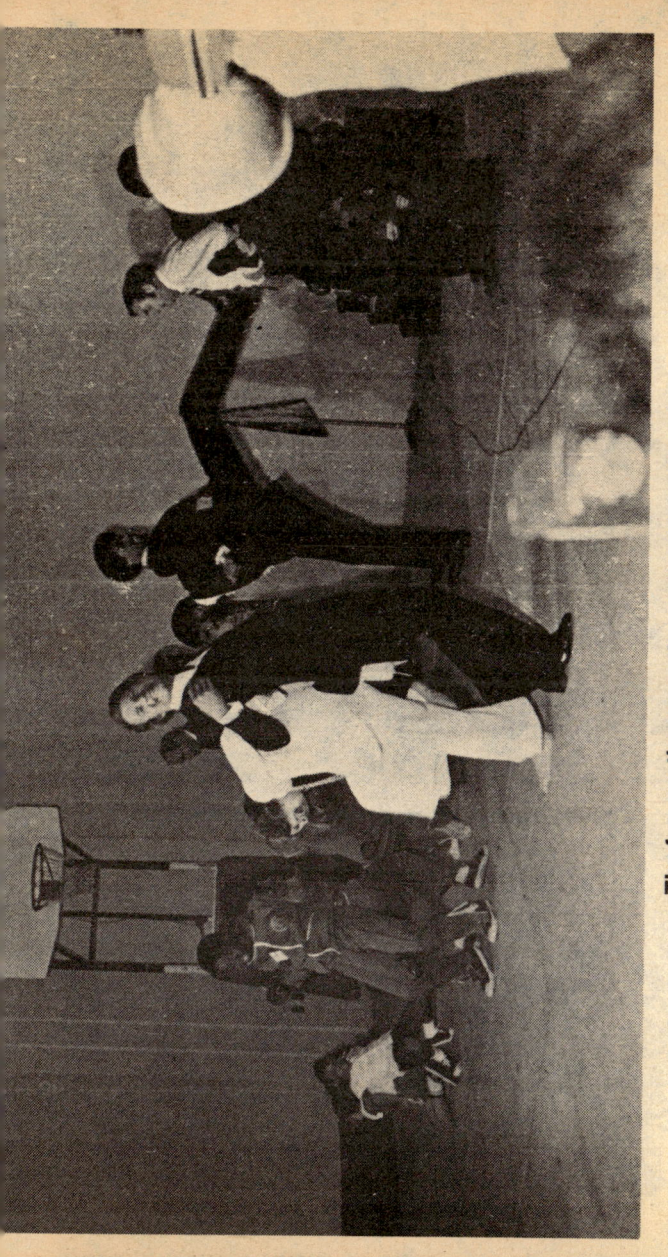

The fun continues as the crew and some of the children join in the action.

It appears as if Frank is asking the First Lady of TV if he can have this dance.

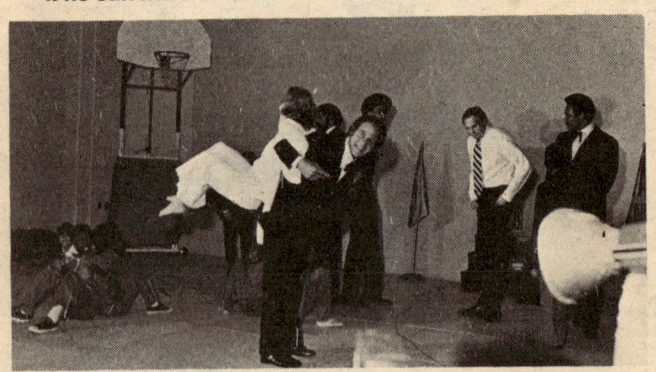

A novel, if unorthodox, dance step that has caught

An usual finale to an original dance step.

Barbara Walters with Sidney Guilikoff at the NBC Affiliate party in Hollywood in May 1973.

The late Frank McGee, respected newscaster and former co-host of the *Today Show* with Barbara Walters.

Irving Mansfield, Jacqueline Susann, Mrs. Earl Wilson and an unidentified guest join Ms. Walters at a Benefit Dinner for the March of Dimes at Mama Leone's.

Stuart Schulberg and Douglas Sinsel accept the 1975 Afternoon TV Magazine Writers and Editors Award for the Best Talk Show Host, awarded jointly to Barbara Walters and Jim Hartz. The *Today Show* also won the award for Best Talk Show. Editor Milburn Smith and writer Deborah Sherwood look on.

despite whatever reservations she may have had—Pat Nixon turned back to public life wholeheartedly, too, and became the most diligent campaigner in the family.

How did the President see the role of political wives in general?

Nixon said he thought every Washington wife had a right to be a personality in her own right, and express her own opinions on public issues if she so chose. But he excluded his own wife from this guarantee of freedom of speech. It could be awkward and detrimental for the First Lady to disagree publicly with the President. There must be only one voice, said Nixon, emanating from the White House. His daughters, though, he admitted, considered themselves exempt from this rule of silence. Pat, fortunately, agreed with him thoroughly. She made it a rule never to speak out on political issues.

What about wives of Cabinet members? (Barbara was obviously trying to get the President to comment on Martha Mitchell, the irrepressibly frank and opinionated wife of then Attorney General John Mitchell.)

But Nixon refused to pass judgment on his lieutenants or their mates. It was enough of a problem trying to handle the members of his own family, he said simply.

Speaking of families, Barbara pressed on —how did the President view the current crisis in the quality of American family life? The rising drug problem? The widespread disaffection with the Vietnam War? The general feelings of alienation and despair? As the nation's leader, what—in his opinion—was the gravest problem confronting the American family today?

Nixon had an answer ready for every point Barbara brought up—or perhaps platitude, rather than answer, might be a better word.

On the subject of drugs, he said that a person doesn't turn to pills, hard stuff or marijuana unless he's basically dissatisfied with his life.

On anti-war sentiment, he reiterated that his administration was working very hard to bring American military involvement in Southeast Asia to a speedy conclusion.

On the worst problem facing family life in America, he diagnosed the real trouble as "a sense of insecurity" that comes from old values being destroyed or discarded.

As for the real solution, the thirty-seventh President of the United States practically borrowed a leaf from Kennedy's 1961 Inaugural Address ("Ask not what your country can do for you—ask what you can do for your country") when he told Barbara Walters that the only cure for personal dissatisfaction was for every citizen to decide what contribution he could best make to society. It is the responsibility of the older generation, said Nixon, to instill in the younger generation a sense of pride— pride in itself and pride in our country.

Looking straight into *Today's* cameras, Nixon made a personal plea to the young people of America not to give up on society, not to be deterred when they see imperfection all around them—but to work within the system to change it, rather than try to destroy it. "What does it prove to shout a slogan?" said Nixon. ". . . What does it prove unless you do something about it . . . something in terms of working with the system to change it?"

Twenty months before the next Presidential election, and fifteen months before the historic Watergate break-in, it seemed at that moment as if Richard M. Nixon was already back on the campaign trail.

And, obviously, he didn't think the support of the younger generation would be crucial to his reelection. For, continuing on the topic of youth, Nixon mentioned to Barbara Walters that college kids standing outside the White House and shouting obsenities were becoming very boring to him. As for marijuana? Well, perhaps, the penalties for smoking pot were too severe in some states and should be lightened—but the use of marijuana should definitely not be legalized.

At that point, with the interview almost over, Barbara Walters moved an eighth of an inch closer to President Nixon on the couch. Practically whispering, she seized the relaxed feeling of the moment to say, "Mr. President, we sit here, you and I, talking . . . I realize there is nothing I can't ask you if I want to. . . ."

Nixon nodded, gently reminding her that that's what he had assured her before the interview started. So, with the definite sensation that she might just have the President of the United States securely in the palm of her hand, Barbara Walters took a deep breath, and asked the question that would go down in history as the juiciest part of her forty-two minutes in the Blue Room.

Barbara: ". . . There has been a lot of talk, Mr. President, about your image and the fact that the American public—forgive me, Mr. President—sees you as rather a stuffy man and not a human man. Are you —oh, dear. Are you worried about your image, Mr. President?"

Nixon: "Not at all. When Presidents begin to worry about images, when they begin to be concerned about polls, when they begin to read their press clippings, do you know what happens? They become like the athletes, the football teams and the rest, who become so concerned about what is said about them that they don't play the game well."

According to Nixon, the man who sits in the Oval Office has too many monumental responsibilities to spend his time preening in front of a mirror, sprucing himself up for public opinion's sake. He reminded Barbara that Winston Churchill had once said, "anybody who takes his temperature with a Gallup Poll isn't going to be a very good leader." So, all in all, Nixon believed that if he had truly worried about his image, chances are he wouldn't be President right now, sitting in the Blue Room of the White House, entertaining Barbara Walters and her *Today* crew. Someone else would.

And so, the interview drew to a well-orchestrated close, with not one false note floating in the air. Nixon's final comment to Barbara, on the theme of image, was—"I am not going to change my image. I am just going to do a good job for this country."

Barbara was pleased with the interview, and so was Nixon. Previously, Barbara had scored points with the First Family by her favorable TV treatment of Tricia, proving that the President's daughter was vitally concerned with more things than just lawn parties and lollipops. But now—following the huge success of her TV chat with the President—her stock at 1600 Pennsylvania Avenue rose even higher.

For her part, Barbara later admitted in *How to Talk with Practically Anybody about Practically Anything* that "I've been charmed by him every time we've met." Her first peek at the President occurred during her White House interview with Tricia. Nixon had emerged from his office briefly to watch the elaborate TV preparations from the sidelines. Barbara took the opportunity to ask Nixon if she could pose for a picture with him (after kissing LBJ on the cheek, she didn't have much shyness left when it came to Presidents). Nixon agreed to the picture-snapping, then gallantly invited her to chat with him in his office for a few minutes. There, he proceeded to disarm her instantly by telling her that she was sitting in the same chair that Golda Meir, the Prime Minister of Israel, had occupied recently. This led Barbara and the President to talk about Israel and Mideast tensions for several minutes. It was at this point, in fact, that Prince Philip's name popped into the conversation, and the President promised Barbara he'd persuade the Prince to come on her show.

Barbara and Nixon met on one more occasion—again briefly—prior to his *Today* stint. She was at the White House, covering a dinner honoring painter Andrew Wyeth. Nixon noticed her, singled her out from a group of female reporters, and again took a few moments to chat with her.

In her book, Barbara candidly admits developing a small crush on Nixon. Contrary to his usual public image, she says she found him handsome, warm-blooded and far more attractive than he comes across in print or on television. "He has sex-appeal—he's slim and suntanned," she writes—all in all, a very sexy and charming gentleman.

Barbara was one of the few members of the news industry who Nixon appeared to trust. It was a position that certainly helped her career, but also had its drawbacks. In September 1972—six months after Barbara had accompanied the Nixons to China—she confided to James Conaway in *The New York Times Magazine*: ". . . I don't want to lose my credentials as a reporter, so I don't want to be identified too closely with the Nixons. Some people think I'm the Nixon girl, the White House pet. That depends on your point of view. Remember, I was the first one to get an interview with Teddy Kennedy after Chappaquiddick."

So much for the Nixons. Is there anyone

left of public note whom Barbara Walters hasn't gotten around to interviewing yet? Probably not. Unless, of course, you're thinking of Howard Hughes or the Abominable Snowman. Barbara once said that when she mentally ticks off all the beautiful, celebrated and powerful people she's encountered on the air, she sometimes thinks she would gladly be *Today's* female star for no money at all. Then, she qualifies that sweeping claim by adding that she used to make that statement all the time, till her first NBC contract came up for renewal. At that point, her agent made her stop announcing she'd forego a salary.

Viewers often wonder which world leader, writer or movie star has made the strongest impression on Barbara Walters—which interview she treasures most. Ironically, the *Today* guest whose presence touched her most deeply was not a celebrated person at all. He was a blind and deaf poet named Robert Smithdas, who teaches similarly handicapped people in Brooklyn, New York. When he was interviewed on the *Today* show, Barbara commucated with him by a special kind of lip reading. He placed his thumb on Babara's lips as she spoke and felt her words. "Of my nearly eleven years of interviewing," Barbara informed *Newsweek* in 1974, "this is the man who has made the most lasting impression." She was mor moved by her conversation with this man than by all her publicized chats with Lyndon Johnson, Richard Nixon, Prince Philip, Dean Rusk, Golda Meir and Mrs. Martin Luther King. She still feels that way today.

CHAPTER VI

Wife and Mother

". . . I don't want a total revolution in the state of women. I like the feminine role. I like being a mother, and having my home revolve primarily around my husband's life."
—Interview with Judy Klemesrud
in **The N.Y. Times**, 1970.

Lee Guber was proud of her success. He lined a whole wall of their West-side Manhattan apartment with photographs of her professional triumphs. For her part, during their marriage, she went to great lengths to assure people that Lee was the breadwinner in the family—accomplished in his own right as a theatrical producer long before they met. And she once wrote, "It is true love when you continue to care for a man who sleeps while you go off to work."

For eight years and seven months, the marriage of Lee Guber and Barbara Walters survived. Then suddenly, in July 1974, it collapsed.

Lee Guber seemed like the perfect mate for Barbara—sophisticated, ambitious, hooked on show business and an even more dazzling impresario than her father. Lee first appeared on the theatrical scene in 1955 when he joined forces with two other

Philadelphians—Shelly Gross and Frank Ford—to start a chain of canvas-topped summer theaters. All three men were in their thirties, astute horsetraders and fascinated by the theater world. Lee was a Doctor of Sociology. Shelly was a Phi Beta Kappa. Frank—the only performer in the trio—was a Philadelphia TV personality, whom the *N.Y. Times* once referred to as "a David Susskind of the Philadelphia air waves."

By 1962, seven years after launching their tent-show operation, Messers Guber, Gross and Ford owned six thriving summer theaters and were recognized in show business circles as the foremost entrepreneurs in the field of outdoor entertainment. Their "Music Fairs"—as their tent theaters were called—were located all along the Eastern seaboard—Westbury, Long Island; Valley Forge, Pa.; Camden, N.J.; West Springfield, Mass.; Painters Mill, Md.; and Washington, D.C. They attracted some of Broadway's biggest stars as headliners. In the summer season of 1962, for example, the Music Fair repertory consisted of fourteen productions—eleven musicals and three comedies—including *Tunnel of Love, Kismet, Bells Are Ringing, Anything Goes* and *Fiorello*. And on the roster of stars were Robert Cummings, George Gobel, Darren

McGavin, Dorothy Collins, Red Buttons and Martha Raye.

1962 was also the year that Guber, Gross and Ford decided to expand operations. They announced plans to open restaurants adjoining their six canvas theaters, and began formulating plans to eventually produce plays on Broadway and on television. There were even—shades of Lou Walters!— plans in the works to enter the nightclub field. The three young Philadelphians were also interested in opening a seventh Music Fair right in the heart of New York City, and were busy negotiating with Freedomland, the gigantic amusement park located in the Bronx, for a possible tent site. But the *Times* reported that negotiations broke down because the park's rental demands were too high. (Life is funny, though. It's interesting to note that today Lee Guber's chain of summer theaters is still going strong, while Freedomland no longer exists. It was torn down to accommodate a mammoth apartment development called Co-op City.)

As a first step toward their multi-media expansion goal, Guber, Gross and Ford incorporated in the early 1960s—and Music Fair Enterprises, Inc. was born. When the corporation was established, one hundred thousand shares of stock were circulated on the market at five dollars apiece, and MFE, Inc. entered into an arrangement with Durgon-Katz Associates to produce musicals and book them for Broadway, hotels, nightclubs and industrial shows. Furthermore, there were sketches on the drawing board to build a wax museum in Philadelphia, near Independence Hall, devoted to great men and great moments in American history.

During the 1960s, Lee Guber established himself as a theatrical heavyweight—the David Merrick of the straw-hat circuit. What was the secret of his success? In a decade when Broadway ticket revenues were rapidly declining, Guber and his two energetic partners accurately gauged that middle-class suburban Americans were hungry for lighthearted, live theater. And their native business intelligence helped a great deal, too. In May 1962, the Philadelphia trio explained to the *N.Y. Times* their formula for making profits. They had learned early in their summer ventures, they said, that they could reduce costs considerably by operating as a chain, instead of focusing their attention on a single theater. So, starting with their second season, they built a new theater every summer. Each of the plays they produced played at all six theaters on a rotating basis. And MFE, Inc. developed its own transport system—chartering buses to move cast, costumes and scenery from tent to tent. Getting top names in the entertainment world to headline their productions helped considerably, too; and Guber, Gross and Ford believed they were able to attract stars because they could offer them a full summer's work in six different theaters, rather than just a two or three week engagement in one place.

With the solid success of the Music Fairs, Lee Guber has turned more of his attention to Broadway over the years. With Shelly Gross (Frank Ford dropped out along the way), he has produced some of the New York theater's splashiest hits of the '70s—Angela Lansbury in *Gypsy*, Carol Channing in *Lorelei*, Jane Powell in *Irene* and Alice Faye in *Good News*. In fact, a recent edition of *Show Business* reports that this year Guber and Gross have turned the actual management of the Music Fairs over to Marty Kummer and Bob Calley, so that they can devote themselves exclusively to Broadway and road-show projects. The G & G team is particularly interested at present in producing a Bicentennial musical for their Valley Forge theater, which is built on an historic Revolutionary battlefield.

It's obvious that in some ways Lee Guber

resembles Barbara's father. Both are showmen with a certain Midas touch. Lou Walters started a successful chain of East Coast nightclubs. Lee Guber runs a chain of East Coast summer theaters. Even their first names—both one syllable, both starting with the same letter—are similar enough to be confused.

Barbara met Lee Guber on a blind date in 1961. She was thirty years old at the time, with one bad marriage behind her, an established *career woman*, hardly panting to give up her independence and success for domestic oblivion. They dated fast, furiously—and non-committedly—for the next two years.

They fought, broke up and reconciled—all the things people in love frequently do. They also had their quieter moments. Once, Barbara gave a birthday party for Lee in her three-room bachelor apartment, and, in the true spirit of Mary Tyler Moore and Marlo Thomas, invited far more people than the apartment could really accommodate. But ingenuity saved the day. A neighbor let Barbara store all her bedroom furniture in her flat, and Barbara rented two round tables and set them up in her bedroom. She also rented two elegant tablecloths to cover the tables, and a sizable number of folding chairs. Then, with a final ingenious flourish that would surely win a merit badge from *Cosmopolitan's* Helen Gurley Brown, Barbara covered her bedroom dresser with yet another rented cloth and—voila!—a serving table! Converting the bedroom into a dining area left the living room completely free for socializing, and the party was a sparkling success. Afterwards, Barbara joked that her cleverness as a hostess that night is what finally convinced Lee to marry her.

As Mrs. Lee Guber, Barbara prided herself on being a competent and creative hostess. On one occasion, however, even her determined efforts couldn't save the party from being a preordained flop. It happened that the Gubers were giving an anniversary party for some friends during the height of one of New York's worst flu epidemics. Originally, twenty guests were invited for dinner, but by the day of the party, so many people had cancelled out due to illness that only twelve sat down to dinner. Even worse, only eleven *finished* dinner! When NBC radio news commentator Ben Grauer had started looking sickly between the soup course and the salad, Barbara had ordered him to lie down in the bedroom. Then, she decided to take his temperature. It registered 103 and the poor man had to leave.

According to James Conaway's article in

The N.Y. Times Magazine, if Lee Guber hadn't proposed, Barbara might have married Roy Cohn, the young lawyer who became known as Senator Joseph McCarthy's right-hand man during the 1950s. Cohn met Barbara at her father's nightclub in Miami. They were introduced by Lou Walters, who apparently told Cohn that Barbara wanted to meet him—"She's a great admirer of yours." Barbara, whose political views already differed considerably from Cohn's, reputedly cut her father short and said, "I wanted to meet you. Period."

Barbara Walters—the woman who found Richard Nixon "a sexy man"—seems to be attracted to men who represent power— whether it's power in the world of show business, Wall Street or politics. And during the 1950s, no young man in Washington was more powerful than Roy Marcus Cohn.

Cohn was the only child of a well-known New York judge, who was closely connected with the Democratic Party. In his 1971 biography of the late Joe McCarthy, *When Even Angels Wept*, Thomas writes that "Roy Cohn had been indulged in every whim by his adoring parents. Them he revered but did not emulate." He attended exclusive private schools, where he gained the reputation for being something of a "whiz kid." He more than lived up to that reputation when he was granted special permission by the headmaster of the Horace Mann School for Boys to speed up his education. With that permission, he finished high school a half-year early and entered Columbia University, where he earned both a bachelor's and a law degree in under four years, mainly by burning the midnight oil and attending summer sessions.

Cohn was graduated from Columbia at twenty, a year too young to be admitted to the bar. Through his father's influence in judicial circles, though, he bided his time working in the United States Attorney's office. Then, Roy turned twenty-one. On the very day he passed his bar exam, he became an assistant U.S. Attorney.

From the start, Roy Cohn was more interested in politics than law, and he maneuvered it so that several headline-making cases came his way. His peculiar specialty, as he himself phrases it in his book *A Fool for a Client*, was as "prosecutor of second-string Communist leaders." He helped draw up the government's indictment against Owen Lattimore; he was associated with the Remington perjury case; and most notably, he was in great measure responsible for the conviction of accused atomic spies Julius and Ethel Rosenberg.

The Rosenbergs eventually went to the

electric chair for their alleged espionage against the United States, but their case was destined to become a *cause celebre*. A whole school of historians has since rushed to their belated defense, arguing that they were improperly tried, then sentenced to death, more because of the hysterical mood of the times than the actual gravity of their crimes. Cohn, however, has steadfastly maintained that justice was not miscarried in the Rosenberg case. "The case itself was dramatic and important, but uncomplicated," he states in *A Fool for a Client*. "The Rosenbergs were deeply committed to Communism."

As the prosecution—and Roy Cohn—viewed it, the thrust of the case was simple and clear-cut. The Rosenbergs were fanatically devoted to the Communist cause. Ethel Rosenberg recruited her brother, David Greenglass, into the couple's undercover activities. While in the Armed Forces, David was stationed in Los Alamos, New Mexico, where portions of the first atomic bomb were being assembled. He managed to secure top-secret information—including actual sketches of the bomb—which he turned over to Julius and Ethel who later forwarded the documents to the Kremlin.

How ironic it was that Roy Cohn—the man who prosecuted the Rosenbergs—came so close to marrying Barbara Walters. For in 1970, Lee Guber, the man Barbara did marry, produced a play on Broadway called *Inquest*, which provoked a storm of controversy in its passionate defense of the Rosenbergs.

The Rosenbergs were convicted in 1951. A year later, Roy Cohn, at the age of 26, was chosen by Senator Joseph McCarthy as chief counsel of his Government Operations Committee, which was seeking to flush out suspected Red sympathizers in every branch of the federal government. Cohn rode high on the crest of McCarthyism while the Senator was in power; but with the decline of McCarthy, Roy Cohn seemed to fade out of sight. Twice during the 1960s, Cohn returned to front-page prominence, less favorably, when he was criminally charged with perjury, bribery and extortion in connection with a stock fraud. But on each occasion he was acquitted. His experiences as a criminal defendant led him to write *A Fool for a Client*, which details his battle to prove his own innocence.

Cohn's relationship with Barbara Walters is probably one of the least known facts about either of them. Cohn has publicly remarked that he was attracted to Barbara because she was independent, yet vulnerable, and had a mind like a steel trap. He admits Barbara never got along with his mother because they were both strong women. Today, Barbara has a copy of *A Fool for a Client* sitting on a shelf in her Rockefeller Center office. Inside, the inscription reads: "For Chickie—who I always knew would accomplish Joe McCarthy's dream of restoring me to daytime television." (Roy Cohn had been a guest on the *Today* show, his first video stint since the celebrated Army-McCarthy hearings were televised in the early 1950s.)

For her part, Barbara Walters has an autographed copy of Roy Cohn's book. His memento from *her* is a letter he received during a particularly bleak period of his life some years ago, when he was struggling to raise money for his own legal defense. "Once, when I was a little discouraged," he reveals in *A Fool for a Client*, "I received a letter telling me to stop feeling sorry for myself and to count these blessings of friendship. It came from Barbara Walters, the pretty young lady whom I knew before she rose to her present unique position on the national airwaves."

Roy Cohn maintains that he proposed to Barbara on December 7, 1963—the night before she married Lee Guber. Barbara denies it. Cohn says, nonetheless, that he spent an hour pleading with her on a restaurant phone to become his wife. She was turning him down, she kept insisting, because she and Lee Guber already had their marriage license and an appointment with a judge. In fact, they had even given the judge a present, ahead of time, for marrying them!

And so, despite Roy Cohn's phone-booth objections, Barbara Walters became Mrs. Lee Guber on December 8, 1963. But at the age of 32—having already traveled to India with Jacqueline Kennedy and just begun to shine on morning television—Barbara was hardly ready to settle into some comfortable surburban mold. Neither, apparently, was Lee Guber. For the first six months of their marriage, both husband and wife continued to maintain their old bachelor apartments. Well, they were hardly run-of-the-mill newlyweds. Indeed, chances are, if the bride and groom had had the courage back then to buck convention, they might never have been newlyweds at all. "We really just wanted to cling together stormily," Barbara later reported to the press. But this was 1963—before living together became a national pastime—and so, Lee and Barbara did the socially acceptable thing, by their generation's standards, and got hitched.

Still, for Barbara and Lee—two fiercely independent people—the hardest adjustment in getting married was, believe it or not, moving in together. By the time August 1973 rolled around and *Washington Post* reporter Sally Quinn was hired as Barbara Walters' competition on *The CBS Morning News*, times had changed radically. Now TV anchor ladies could make love with whomever they wanted, and not worry about marriage at all. A month before coming on CBS, Sally Quinn revealed to *New York Magazine* that she was planning to room with her longtime boyfriend Warren Hoge, city editor of *The New York Post*. Sally and Warren had once been engaged, but three days before the wedding, Sally had thrown all the stuffed animals Warren had given her in his face, and called the whole thing off. Now they were happier—just commuting back and forth between Washington and New York to see each other. But would Sally's move to New York—and into Warren's apartment—change all that? "When Sally got the CBS offer," *New York Magazine* reported, "she and Warren had a long talk about whether he wanted her to live with him. He said that he did. They hope that it will not be as bad as being engaged."

But back in 1963, Barbara Walters and Lee Guber couldn't take life as blithely. They got their blood tests and marriage license first, and only then signed the lease on a joint apartment. Then, in the seventh month of their marriage, they actually began "living together." It was a sensible, seven-room apartment on Manhattan's West 57th Street.

Barbara set out to decorate the apartment with two ideas in mind—she wanted to make it lively and comfortable. The living room was done in bright red. "There is no place where you can't put your feet up," Barbara once informed a reporter from *House Beautiful*. The living room sometimes doubled as Lee's second business office so the setting had to be sturdy but casual. He would sometimes hold auditions there. Then, on quiet evenings at home, the living room was also the place where Lee and Barbara would read or talk.

Why red? "I think red is a warm color, like Christmas," Barbara explained when *House Beautiful* came to see for themselves in October 1970. "And I'm a brunette and I look good in it." When the Gubers first decided on a red decorating scheme for their living room, Barbara admitted she had been slightly doubtful about the overall effect. Would it be too loud and gaudy? But, when all was said and done, she was rather pleased with it. "I like my home," she told the readers of *House Beautiful*, and it all looks so pretty, I think, 'Isn't this a pretty room!' I'm always happy to come home to it. I thought I'd be sick of the red in three months, but it's been six years, and I still love it."

Along with comfort, a tranquil mood was the keynote of the Guber living room. Barbara wanted a feeling of serenity to permeate, so the walls were painted white to soften the dominant red of the furniture. Elegant draperies gave the room a soft, flowing look, also tempering the red, but serving another, less obvious purpose as well. They made great storage space. Behind them, Barbara kept several little circular tables which she used for entertaining. The furniture itself was a happy blend of traditional and ultra-modern.

Red, Barbara's favorite color, didn't cover all the walls and floors of the Guber apartment, but it did make its presence felt rather strongly. Even the kitchen was red. It was a large, old-fashioned room with exposed pipes butting against the latest, up-to-the-minute appliances. It had red ceiling, red countertops, red pots and pans. More toned-down, however, were the master bedroom and daughter Jacqueline's nursery, both of which were done in very sunny yellow. Barbara chose yellow for the room she and Lee shared because, she explained to

House Beautiful, "it's a color that doesn't look too feminine."

There's something solid and permanent about furnishing a seven-room apartment in New York's Central Park district, yet "solid" and "permanent" are words that Barbara would probably cringe to hear describe her lifestyle. Perhaps, deep inside, she's never quite lost the wanderlust that was an involuntary part of her childhood. It gives her a feeling of casualness about possessions. She could never be the kind of person who worries about her paintings or her diamonds or her fur coats—the kind of person who must be surrounded by beautiful things. Yet, the thought of living out of a suitcase, moving from one hotel to another, doesn't much appeal to her, either. Perhaps, there are really two Barbara Walters. One is a tough, single-minded TV reporter, ready to fly off to Sydney, Australia at a moment's notice if Judge Crater ever popped up there. The other is the good Jewish girl from Sarah Lawrence who really wants two cars in the driveway, the Tudor house, the tousled kids, the dental checkups with no cavities.

When Judy Klemesrud interviewed Barbara for the August 29, 1970 edition of *The N.Y. Times,* the two women naturally got around to discussing women's liberation—

what else? Barbara told Ms. Klemesrud that she definitely favors improving the economic and social plight of women—she's all for more day-care centers and employment opportunities (she also later came out for legalized abortion)—but she didn't agree with some of the more radical theories of the movement. For one thing, she didn't want to see a radical upheaval in traditional family life. ". . . I don't want a total revolution in the state of women," announced one of America's most independent, ambitious women. "I like the feminine role. I like being a mother, and having my home revolve primarily around my husband's life."

And for the first six years of marriage, before Barbara added *Not For Women Only* to her daily TV workload, went to China with the Nixons, and gradually became a forty-year-old superstar, her home did revolve around her husband's life. The Gubers ate dinner when Lee came home from the theater or office—late in the evening—and even though, she'd be up at 4:30 again the next morning, Barbara would never dream of eating earlier so she could go to bed. Only when Lee was away on business trips could Barbara allow herself the luxury of curling under the covers soon after it was lights out for Jacqueline, and just catching up on her reading.

It was definitely an unusual marital situation. The wife, a national TV star whose day began promptly at 4:30 a.m. The husband, a well-known theatrical producer whose day never ended before eight p.m. How did it ever work at all? (Or, as one mutual friend of the Gubers once observed, "No wonder they maintained separate apartments for the first six months of their marriage—they didn't want to wake each other up coming and going!")

Barbara used to be fond of saying that their marriage was strengthened by the fact that they were both connected with show business. They understood each other's needs, and more importantly, were tolerant of each other's time schedules. "I think we give each other a kind of freedom and respect," was how she characterized their relationship for *House Beautiful.* Still, you can't have everything. "It's all very hard," she added in the same interview, "and it takes an exceptional job and an intelligent, understanding husband to make it worthwhile. . . . Lee doesn't mind going to the movies alone and doesn't expect souffles. Somehow it all works."

And in the 1973 *New York Magazine* piece on Barbara's new rival for ratings, Sally Quinn, Lee Guber made this statement about life with *Today's* woman: "I must have known what kind of woman I wanted to be married to. She's not the kind of woman not to be committed or involved. My involvement with her career is slight. I've helped guide her to the right managers, and I watch her most mornings unless she's got four women showing crewel work."

Throughout the last five years, whatever the strains on her marriage (and there, obviously, must have been strains for some time), there has been one constant source of pride, joy and fulfillment in Barbara's personal life—her daughter, Jacqueline, whom she adopted after suffering three miscarriages. Like Marilyn Monroe (who was never able to bear a child) and Sophia Loren (who endured one tragic pregnancy after another before finally becoming a mother), Barbara's maternal drive was as strong as her quest for stardom, perhaps even more so. Just how much she longed to be a parent is illustrated by the anecdote she frequently tells about the tactless man she once encountered at a cocktail party. As Barbara tells it, some years ago she was introduced to a very pleasant man at a party who immediately announced that he was a big fan of hers. In fact, he rarely missed an episode of the *Today* program and, he said, had watched the show with increasing enthusiasm when Barbara was pregnant. He was overjoyed the day she announced the birth of her baby on the air. Friends of Ms. Walters who happened to be present, knowing Barbara's tragic maternity record and that Jacqueline is adopted, cringed at the man's thoughtlessness, unintentional though it may have been. But Barbara herself knew the man spoke purely from ignorance. She regretted only that he would feel badly if and when he discovered his embarrassing *faux pas*.

Still, after waiting so long for motherhood (Jacqueline didn't arrive on the scene until Barbara was in her late thirties), Barbara would never dream of giving up her career to be a full-time, twelve-hour-a-day kind of mother. Not that she thinks that non-working mothers are either more or less successful raising children than working mothers are. Speaking only for herself, Barbara believes that the present arrangement—programming time for work and time for Jacqueline—is the best possible alternative. After all, when Barbara is with her child, she is totally involved with her, playing with her, doing things with her, concentrating on her. Jacqueline's time doesn't get interrupted by phone calls or doorbells ringing or a thousand and one other disturbances that normally take non-working mothers away from their children.

Of course, no matter how tightly you plan and program your life, there are only so many hours in each day. Compromises occasionally have to be made, plans scratched and appointments cancelled. Until 1972, at least, Barbara seemed to have a wise and successful philosophy where her home life versus her working life was concerned. She felt in each instance you choose what you're going to do, and then you must be prepared to make sacrifices. It's simply a matter of priorities. If she decided that she wanted to keep Wednesday afternoon completely free to take Jacqueline to see a Disney movie, then all her film editing and research might have to get squeezed into Tuesday—somehow. It might mean skipping a luncheon date on Tuesday to do it, but then the time gained with Jacqueling on Wednesday would more than make up for it. The important thing, Barbara repeatedly maintained, was that once the choice was made—whether to be with her child or get away for the weekend with her husband or play badminton with Andy Warhol and Marion Javits—it was irrevocable. There was no room for reevaluating to the point of neurosis.

That philosophy seemed to work very well until her marriage ended suddenly in

1972. Was her TV career to blame? A year earlier, Barbara had cancelled a Palm Springs vacation with Lee for a chance to interview President Nixon; that same year, she had taken on, in addition to her *Today* status, the job of moderating *Not For Women Only*; and she seemed to be traveling to distant parts of the globe more than ever before to get her stories. Something had to give. And something did. When *the* choice had to be made, Barbara Walters—the woman who had it all under control—the wife who used to specify at dinner parties that her place card read "Mrs. Lee Guber" or "Barbara Walters Guber"—she chose what she apparently really wanted—to be single again.

After the separation, she began dating. Her first dinner partner was a well-known producer of TV panel and game shows. Then came wine shipper Alexis Lichine and businessman Everett Kovler. In 1974, she insisted to *Newsweek* that there was no man in her life on a serious basis. But she felt more secure about her career and, therefore, about her life. "I've stopped worrying that it's all going to end tomorrow," was how she described her new-found feeling of inner calm, and writer Elizabeth Peer was forced to agree. Barbara Walters in 1974, two years after the failure of her second marriage, was obviously glowing. Said Ms. Peer: "Whether the catalyst is motherhood fulfilled or success—or her separation from Guber, as some friends speculate—Barbara Walters is conspicuously happy these days."

Although the actual breakup didn't occur until 1972, in retrospect it seems probable that there were tensions in the Guber household long before that. And if there were battles going on at home, by 1970 Lee Guber was also having his share of battles on the theatrical front. For in that year, he produced *Inquest* on Broadway—a play that generated a torrent of political fireworks, and in a very ironic way suddenly pitted Lee Guber against Barbara's old flame, Roy Cohn.

Inquest—A Tale of Political Terror opened on Broadway in May 1970. Written by Donald Freed and directed by Alan Schneider, it starred George Grizzard and Anne Jackson in a pseudo-documentary, ultra-sympathetic portrait of Julius and Ethel Rosenberg. The play made a strong plea for the Rosenbergs' innocence, nearly twenty years after the fact. Several critics took stern exception to the premise of *Inquest*. One of them, Walter Goodman, contributed an article to the May 24th issue of *The New York Times Magazine*, denouncing

Inquest for possibly distorting history as much in the Rosenbergs' favor as their actual trial may have been distorted against them.

Three weeks later, Lee Guber's and Shelly Gross' printed response to Goodman appeared in the magazine's letters-to-the-editor section. In his rebuttal, Guber maintained that *Inquest* had not been produced to prove the innocence of the Rosenbergs. At the same time (this was three months after Barbara's China trip with the Nixons) he took the opportunity to condemn the rise of "the new opinion suppressors," so reminiscent of the McCarthy witch hunters of the 1950s. Lee Guber's mention of "the new opinion suppressors" was obviously a veiled reference to the Nixon Administration's determination to sabotage the press.

According to Guber, the Rosenbergs, as delineated in *Inquest*, were merely symbols in an allegory. "We were doing a play about injustice," he emphasized in the *Times*. "We wanted to show that, given a special political climate, in this or any other country, the probabilities of a fair trial are diminished, if not eliminated." In other words, *Inquest* was simply about a very basic and timeless theme—the danger of public hysteria destroying democracy. It should be viewed in the same light as Arthur Miller's *The Crucible* and Ibsen's *An Enemy of the People*.

Actually, if the author and producers were concerned about any historical period at all, it was our own age—the Nixon Era. "We felt," wrote Guber and Gross, "*Inquest* was a passion play that should be done in a democracy every decade. As we hear and read the words of the new opinion suppressors, we are reinforced in our belief. Once again, we see the first bitter buds of McCarthyism finding eager gardeners."

It certainly came as no surprise to Lee Guber that Roy Cohn was not among *Inquest's* admirers. Having been a member of the prosecuting team that helped send the Rosenbergs to the death chamber, Cohn may have viewed the play as, in some measure, a personal attack on him. In *A Fool for a Client*, he provides his own critique of *Inquest*, claiming—from the standpoint of someone intimately connected with the trial —that the play distorted history by omitting several major pieces in the Rosenberg puzzle. *Inquest* did not mention, for example, the whole business of the passport pictures. After the Rosenbergs had denied under oath having taken passport photos in an attempt to flee the country, the photographer they'd used appeared to testify against them. Also, according to Cohn, the play neglected to note that the United States Court of Appeals upheld the couple's conviction and that the Supreme Court rejected seven appeals on their behalf.

But, in this half-personal, half-political battle with Lee Guber, Roy Cohn seemed piqued for yet an entirely different reason. It had to do with a cancelled appointment. In the 1970 Broadway production, the part of U.S. Attorney Roy Cohn was portrayed by a young Israeli actor named Michael Bursten. He wrote to Cohn, and the two men made arrangements to meet in person (obviously, Bursten thought it might help his interpretation of the role to meet the flesh-and-blood Roy Cohn). "But," writes Cohn, "he was ordered to cancel the appointment by the show's 'higher-ups.' I guess they wanted to avoid any accuracies that might creep into the show."

In 1970, Barbara Walters' life had come full-circle. Here was her husband, Lee Guber, producing a play intimately involving her old boyfriend, Roy Cohn, while Barbara herself was busy covering every detail in the present life of another Cohn compatriot, Richard Nixon. *Today's* woman was more than just reporting history now—her own life was becoming an integral part of it!

CHAPTER VII

World Traveler

"... *NBC's Barbara Walters, who will concentrate on covering Mrs. Nixon's travels, is concerned that she may have to leave her curlers behind...*"

—**Newsweek**, February 21, 1972, discussing the forthcoming Nixon trip to China.

In March 1962, when she was still a backstage scriptwriter, Barbara Walters did her first overseas assignment for the *Today* show. She accompanied First Lady Jacqueline Kennedy on a grand tour of India and Pakistan.

In India, Barbara stood by while Jackie got her first glimpse of the world's most beautiful building—the Taj Mahal. Later, Barbara faithfully reported Jackie's awed reaction to this magnificent landmark, and passed along to *Today's* viewers such historical tidbits as the fact that the Taj Mahal had been erected by a seventeenth-century Mogul emperor as a tribute to his wife.

There were other memorable moments, too, as Barbara tagged after the First Lady of the United States. There were the incredible throngs of people who jammed every street along the First Lady's route, shouting "Mrs. Kennedy Zindabad!" (Mrs. Kennedy Long Life!). There was the visit to Mahatma Gandhi's memorial to leave a bunch of white roses; time out to feed bananas to Prime Minister Nehru's baby elephant and bamboo shoots to his Himalayan pandas; a motorboat ride down the mystic River Ganges where thousands of Hindus bathed in the sacred waters and endless rows of funeral pyres smoked along the banks.

There was even a heartwarming mishap to report back to *Today's* fans. During her first weekend in India, Mrs. Kennedy was the houseguest of the Maharajah of Udaipur. In her curving white marble bedroom at the Maharajah's lakeside palace, Jackie wrote postcards home to Caroline and John, Jr. She gave them to Ambassador John Kenneth Galbraith to mail for her. In the excitement of managing her trip, however, he completely lost track of the postcards and they stayed in his coat pocket. A few days later, he discovered them and, by way of public confession, made a sheepish display of them to the press.

One of the greatest events in international television coverage was the 1969 investiture of Prince Charles of Wales—and Barbara, of course, was on the scene for NBC. The ancient ceremony at the Welsh castle of Caernarvon took place on July 1, 1969—the same month that marked the landing of the first Americans on the moon. An estimated half a billion people around the world watched on television as twenty-year-old Charles Philip Arthur George Windsor knelt on a slab of Welsh rock, and swore the centuries-old oath of fealty to his mother, Queen Elizabeth II: "I Charles, Prince of Wales, do become your liege man of life and limb and of earthly worship, and faith and trust I will bear unto you to live and die against all manner of folks." With those words, Charles assumed the title of the Prince of Wales—making him titular head of nearly three million Welshmen.

At Caernarvon, Barbara Walters found herself surrounded by four thousand lords, ladies, members of Parliament, clerics and even one archdruid. Despite the turnout, however, the ceremony itself was a brisk sixty minutes and Charles' uncle, the Earl of Snowden (who served as chief scenic designer) managed to bring the show in for about half the one million dollars that was spent in 1911 on investing the last prince of wales—the future Edward VIII (now Duke of Windsor). Why the financial squeeze? Perhaps because in 1969, it was obvious that England was embarked on a royal austerity program. (Barbara passed on to

Today viewers, for example, the news that the little red chairs used by guests at the investiture were actually up for sale. To recoup some of their outlay, Buckingham Palace had decreed that ticket holders could take home their chairs, if they were willing to pay $28.80 each for them.)

Yet, at a time when Queen Liz and Prince Philip were reputedly having trouble balancing the palace checkbook, Charles' investiture was still a bit of a spree. His coronet, especially designed to tone down his large ears, cost $48,000. And the security arrangements at Caernarvon, due to bitter antagonism in certain parts of Wales to the whole event, had to be equally lavish. All in all, two thousand policemen and twenty-five hundred soldiers poured into Caernarvon on that historic, pageant-filled day. Overhead, helicopters maintained a constant surveillance, and frogmen circles the royal yacht, *Britannia*, anchored nearby. Early in the day, there were several bomb threats, and the whole area had to be searched thoroughly. Even the band members of the Welsh Guard and the BBC Welsh Orchestra weren't immune from the bomb search—they had to surrender their trombones and violins for careful scrutiny.

There was good reason for strict security precautions. Welsh nationalists had made no secret of their hatred of the British royal family. As Queen Elizabeth rode to Caernarvon in an open carriage, an egg splashed across the coach door, nearly hitting her in the face. The night before the investiture, two men were killed when a bomb they were planting at Caernarvon went off accidentally. (Still, if the Welsh seem a wee bit anxious for home rule, they are not without justification in their anti-British sentiment. For many years, the British suppressed the Welsh language and culture. Even today, with unemployment so high in Wales, many nationalists feel that they don't get their fair share in roads, housing and social welfare appropriations from Britain.)

The Welsh have been skeptical about being saddled with an English prince as their liege for seven centuries. In 1282, when the last Welsh ruler—Llywelyn ap Gruffyd—was slain by the partisans of Edward I, Edward promised them a new prince who would be born in Wales and could speak no English. But when he actually presented them with the new prince, it turned out to be his own baby son, Edward II, who had just been born at Caernarvon.

For the investiture of Prince Charles, however, Barbara reported on NBC, a great attempt was made not to wound native feelings. Prince Charles prepared for the occasion by studying the Welsh language for nine weeks. The official program of the pageant was printed in two languages—Welsh and English. The Archdruid of Wales took charge of the prayers at the ceremony. And Charles himself, speaking in Welsh to his new subjects, noted that Wales had given the world "many brave men, princes, poets, bards, scholars, and more recently, a very memorable Goon. . . ." (he was referring to comedian Harry Secombe). The twenty-year-old prince (whose income now in 1975 is $480,000 annually—about $80,000 higher than Barbara Walters') may not have thrilled viewers and changed history quite as much as the first men on the moon did later that month, but he did prove a valuable publicity asset when it came to promoting the British monarchy.

The twenty-fifth hundredth anniversary of the founding of the Persian Empire was another affair altogether. While the British royal family had sought to trim the costs of Prince Charles' investiture, the Shah of Iran spared no expense for his country's birthday. In October 1971, Barbara Walters led the team of NBC reporters who flew to Iran to cover the event, and what she witnessed was possibly the most lavish carnival in modern times. The anniversary party—hold on a 160-acre desert near the ancient ruins of Persepolis—lasted four days and nights. On hand were world leaders from sixty-nine countries, including Red China. The impressive guest list included one emperor, a Roman Catholic cardinal, eight kings, and assorted sheiks, presidents, prime ministers, grand dukes and crown princes. The United States sent Vice President Spiro T. Agnew and his wife. Even in October, though, desert temperatures, soaring to 102 degrees by day and dipping to 28 degrees by night, were hardly conducive to entertaining on a grand scale, so the guests were luxuriously housed in fifty air-conditioned tents. And to help them forget the harsh realities of the desert weather, they dined on roast peacock and drank Chateau Lafite Rothschild, 1945.

Aside from celebrating the nation's anniversary, the Shah's party commemorated two other major events—his own thirty-year mark as Iran's potentate and his wife's thirty-third birthday. To salute all three occasions properly, the fifty-two year old Shah Mohammed Reza Pahlavi and his Empress Farah Dibah ordered gold-threaded uniforms for the members of the royal court (the uniforms cost a thousand dollars apiece) and colored light bulbs totaling up to the staggering sum of $840,000. But the

Shah's birthday party also prompted needed social improvements, too—new roads, schools, luxury hotels, the creation of a symphony orchestra and the ground-laying of a hundred thousand seat stadium in Teheran. In an even more far-reaching act of imperial benevolence, the Shah granted amnesty to five thousand prisoners.

Still, the party didn't pass without causing some hard feelings. At the same time that the Shah was pardoning five thousand convicts, two thousand others were being arrested for publicly voicing their disapproval of the grand event. To make sure that dissident factions would have no chance of spoiling the festivities, the party grounds were roped off by miles of barbed wire. Guards bearing submachine guns were stationed all along the perimeter. Was this any way to run a birthday party? While visiting dignitaries sat on silk-upholstered chairs watching 6,200 marchers pass by, depicting ten dynasties of Persian history, the University of Teheran had to be closed to prevent riots. But the Shah and his beautiful empress seemed oblivious to these dark footnotes. At the end of the four-day gala, he felt his purpose had been accomplished. And just what was that purpose? "To reawaken the people of Iran to their past and reawaken the world to Iran."

Four months after her Arabian idyll came an even more fantastic jaunt for Barbara Walters. She was one of a select number of reporters chosen to accompany President Nixon on his historic "journey of peace" to China. Barbara's specific assignment was to cover Mrs. Nixon's activities during the tour. Altogether, the Nixons were accompanied by eighty-seven representatives of the news media, but this number included photographers, cameramen and technicians. The actual number of journalists was far less—twenty-two newspaper writers, eighteen radio and TV commentators, six wire service reporters, six magazine writers and two syndicated columnists, William F. Buckley, Jr. and Joseph Kraft.

Certain newspapers, such as Long Island's *Newsday*, balked at finding themselves excluded from the Nixon China party. Of course, the eighty-seven media people chosen were among two thousand press applicants asking to go; so, even though *Newsday*'s circulation may be larger than six of the newspapers represented, it was obvious that the Nixon Administration just couldn't accommodate everyone. (Print journalists were particularly up in arms about the fact that of "the lucky eighty-seven," forty-three were radio and TV people. CBS' Walter Cronkite didn't think the

Nixons were prejudiced against newspaper and magazine reporters, however, and offered one theory why so many broadcasters were asked along. Cronkite, who happened to be going to Peking himself, declared that TV is "a cumbersome medium." It takes three or four TV people, counting cameramen and technicians, to cover the same story as well as one newspaper reporter.

The Nixon party was slated to arrive in Peking at 11:30 a.m. on February 21, 1972. Weeks before, newcasters and reporters started an intensive program to bone up on the world's least understood country. In one week alone, for example, a Columbia University professor of Chinese civilization estimated that he privately briefed at least thirty journalists. Veteran correspondent Helen Thomas, who would represent United Press International in China, was busy reading John K. Fairbanks' *The United States and China*; other reporters, meanwhile, were thumbing through Edgar Snow's *Red China Today* and Nagel's *Guide to China*.

While trying to give herself an instant Chinese education, Barbara Walters had other things to worry about. What to wear, for example. Barbara had heard that the ABC-TV news crew was taking along ski jackets, waterproof boots and stocking masks to protect themselves against the Chinese cold. *Newsweek* reported that, while other journalists were frantically trying to stuff their suitcases with an adequate supply of cigarettes, Scotch and toilet paper, "NBC's Barbara Walters, who will concentrate on covering Mrs. Nixon's travels, is concerned that she may have to leave her hair curlers behind but is counting on taking several long skirts." (One of the foremost members of the Nixon press party, Theodore H. White, author of *Thunder Out of China*, thought all this frenzied suitcase stuffing was futile. All he planned to take along, he announced, was his razor, toothbrush and some long winter underwear because, said White, Peking in February is no worse than New Hampshire at primary time.)

The American press contingent actually arrived in Peking a little early—on Sunday evening, February 19, Chinese time. They were met by a handful of Chinese officials, and the first thing Barbara Walters noticed was that the male and female officials were dressed exactly alike—Mao jackets, navy blue pants and overcoats, no frills or adornments. It all had the definite look of a military uniform minus stripes and bars.

Barbara was introduced to her interpreter, Miss Tang, an unsmiling, serious-minded woman in her early thirties who looked forty. Despite the fact that she was called "Miss," Barbara soon learned that her interpreter was married and had a two-and-a-half year old daughter. In China, married women keep their maiden name and do not wear wedding rings. Barbara mentioned her own three-year-old daughter, Jacqueline, who was home in New York. Miss Tang said that her daughter lived at a day care center, and she visited her only on weekends.

Barbara found her hotel room surprisingly congenial and comfortable. It came equipped with everything from bedside comb and brush to a constant supply of tangerines. The downstairs restaurant stayed open day and night. Every room had a big, spacious bathtub and, aside from the fact that there were no showers, as innkeepers the Chinese were definitely on par with Conrad Hilton.

On Monday, her first day in Peking, Barbara Walters started off with a Chinese breakfast—egg roll, chicken noodle soup, cold meats and vegetables. Then, since Mrs. Nixon had no scheduled plans for the afternoon, Barbara decided to do some sightseeing of her own. She headed for the Number One Department Store, which she later dubbed "the Macy's of Peking." She was most impressed by the fact that shoes there sold for $1.50 a pair, but the store's ambience left something to be desired. In the middle of winter, it was heated by a single coal stove located near the entrance doorway. Next door to "the Macy's of Peking," however, was a pharmacy and Barbara decided to take a peek in there, too. She was amazed to find the store selling white acupuncture dolls, made out of plastic, with markings on the limbs and torso where needles could be inserted. She was even more amazed to see aphrodisiacs on sale. It seemed strangely out of kilter with the current Chinese national image—prudish, authoritarian, practically asexual.

Barbara's first live broadcast came on Monday night when President Nixon was guest of honor at a state banquet in Peking's Great Hall of the People. Nixon and Premier Chou En-lai exchanged glittering toasts and a Chinese military band serenaded the President with renditions of "Hone on the Range" and "America the Beautiful." It was the one time during the Nixon trip that the thirteen-hour time difference between Peking and New York worked out to NBC's advantage. The banquet took place at 8 p.m. China time, which was 7 a.m. New York time, and the festivities at the Great Hall were carried live right on the *Today* show.

After Monday evening's triumph, Barbara spent Tuesday keeping close tabs on Pat Nixon. She followed her to the kitchen of the Peking Hotel where the First Lady sampled gourmet Chinese delicacies; then to a glass-making factory where Mrs. Nixon picked up a few points to pass on to feminists in America:Chinese male and female workers receive equal salaries for equal work; most working women place their children in day care centers; they get fifty-seven paid days of maternity leave; couples rely on birth control pills and legal abortions to plan their families (two children per family is the social norm).

While touring the glass factory, Barbara managed to strike up a conversation with one of the interpreters. She had just learned that, although it's legal in China to marry at 18, Chairman Meo says men should marry at 28 and women at 25 so they can give more service to their country at an early age. So she asked the interpreter if people marry for love in China. His answer was no. Couples keep company for a year or two, he told her, then marry if they find themselves "politically compatible." Drug stores may sell aphrodisiacs, but Communism has made the Chinese far more pruitanical than Westerners where affairs of the heart are concerned—and romance is all but non-existent. As proof of this, Barbara Walters observed that premarital sex is rare among young Chinese, and that people don't go to the movies to see thrilling love stories. They go, she quipped in *Ladies Home Journal*, to see exotic feature films like "Boy Loves Tractor."

Tuesday evening Barbara accompanied the Nixons back to the Great Hall of the People to view a government-sponsored ballet performance, *The Red Detachment of Women*, which depicted the Red Army's victory over Chiang Kai-Chek's "greedy capitalist" forces in the Chinese civil war. The ballet was produced under the aegis of Mao Tse-tung's present (and fourth) wife, Chiang Ch'ing, herself one of the most powerful figures in the Peking government. As a young actress, she met Meo when the Communists were still busy fleeing the Nationalists. After the Communist takeover in the 1940s, Chiang Ch'ing remained a relatively obscure figure; but during the Cultural Revolution of the 1960s, she rose to prominence, revamping and rewriting the entire repertoire of Chinese opera and ballet. Popular European works, such as *Swan Lake*, were banned from the Chinese stage —only productions with government-approved themes could be performed from then on.

So much for Barbara Walters' brush with Communist Chinese culture. On Wednesday, it was back to social observation again, this time accompanying Pat Nixon to the Evergreen People's Commune, a mammoth collective farm housing forty thousand inhabitants. Mrs. Nixon, sticking to things she knew best such as schools, hospitals and kitchens, visited a classroom on the commune where the children performed specially prepared skits for her. She toured the Evergreen infirmary where a 68-year-old woman was receiving acupuncture treatments for poor circulation. Mrs. Nixon saw the needles stuck into the old woman's limbs, and asked how the treatment was helping her. The old woman told the First Lady, acupuncture helped her stand up in the kitchen to do her cooking.

That afternoon Barbara scored a journalistic coup that put NBC's coverage of the Nixon trip over the top. She obtained exclusive permission to interview one of the families on the Evergreen commune. The family she interviewed was named Kang. It consisted of a 60-year-old father, a 57-year-old mother, and a married 28-year-old daughter. The Kangs had farmed this land for five generations, long before the Communists came to power, but Mrs. Kang felt her lot was far better than that of her ancestors. She remembered from her own childhood how people used to starve to death when the crops froze in the winter. Since the Communists took over, no one starved to death anymore. And although the Kangs' tiny two-room farmhouse (which they now owned) has mud floors, no ice-box or indoor toilet, the Kangs have other prize possessions—tokens of service to the state: a radio, and, on the wall, a framed government citation, saluting their daughter for helping to build a canal on the commune.

On Thursday, Barbara followed the Nixons on another sight-seeing jaunt—this time to view the world-famous twenty-two-hundred year-old Great Wall, which had been built in ten months by Chinese workers to keep out northern invaders. The wall runs fifteen hundred miles long, about the distance from California to Nebraska. Standing at this historic testament to man's architectural genius, Mr. Nixon strove for some historic remark of his own. He said, "We do not want walls of any kind between peoples."

Thursday night Barbara and all the other American correspondents were treated to a Peking duck dinner by the Chinese press. She later recalled that she was enjoying the sugar-coated roasted duck immensely until a Chinese journalist asked her how she was enjoying the duck's webbed feet. She completely lost her appetite.

On Friday there was a quick visit to Peking University; then Friday night, the entire Nixon party, with Barbara clutching a tape recorder, motion picture camera and four boxes of souvenirs, flew to Hangchow. This city, once noted for its beautiful silk and fine tea, is a living picture postcard with its shimmering lakes, ancient tamples and gleaming pagodas. One look and Barbara dubbed it "the Venice of China."

On Saturday night there was yet another banquet, this time replete with Hangchow roast chicken, chrysanthemum cakes and ham soup with scallops on the menu. After dinner, President Nixon introduced various members of the American press to Premier Chou En-lai. Referring to Helen Thomas, he joked, "She's been covering the White House for sixty years." Everyone smiled at that one—the Premier, the President and even Helen herself. Then it was Barbara's tern to take a ribbing. "And this is Barbara Walters," said Nixon to Chou, "We're just breaking her in!"

On Sunday came the Nixon party's third and last stop, Shanghai. With its skyscrapers, smokestacks and brisk cosmopolitan air, Barbara almost felt inclined to dub it "the New York of China." Nixon visited the Shanghai Industrial Center, and Barbara spent the afternoon at the Shanghai Cultural Palace with the First Lady. Here two thousand Shanghai youngsters congregate after school each day to study such culturally approved subjects as ballet, table tennis, painting and model ship building. It was the last stop on the hectic Nixon agenda. After eight whirlwind days in China, Barbara had done everything with America's First Family from feeding pandas in the Peking Zoo and visiting the tombs of the Ming dynasty to touring the celebrated Forbidden City. Now she reported home to NBC viewers the Nixons' farewell gift to Chairman Mao and the Chinese people— "Birds of Peace"—exquisitely sculptured porcelain swans designed as a symbol of peace and friendship between the two countries.

But although her trip to China was eye-opening and informative, Barbara Walters returned home to the United States with several misgivings. In *Ladies Home Journal*, she noted that she was dismayed at the severe "mental conformity" she had seen all around her in China and at the lack of beauty and creative art. She mentioned that the Pan-American stewardesses on the flight home, with their lipstick, eyeshadow and deep suntans, looked like Playboy bunnies next to the drab Chinese women. Possibly the best part of the trip for her came a half hour out of Shanghai airport, heading back to New York. That's when the hot dogs and hamburgers were served.

If Barbara Walters came home from China slightly disappointed by the lifestyle she saw there, her eighty-six press companions were even more disillusioned. They complained bitterly about the lack of hard news available during this historic "journey of peace." There seemed to be a total news blackout surrounding the President's summit meetings with Chinese leaders. What the newscasters—and the American public, in turn—were getting fed to them, instead, were hotel kitchen tours with Pat Nixon and trips to the Chinese ballet with the President. NBC commentator John Chancellor summed up the press' anger and frustration when he said, "The American people are being treated, in terms of information given to them, like the Chinese people. They are getting no real information at all."

Despite all the hoopla, however, Americans seemed genuinely disappointed with network TV coverage of the Nixon journey. It wasn't anybody's fault, of course, but simply the fact that Richard Nixon's internationally-televised trek to Red China somehow lacked anything approaching real excitement. Barbara Walters found the atmosphere at Peking's airport on the morning of the Nixon arrival dreary and faintly disappointing. She told NBC viewers she had expected a marching band replete with cymbals clashing and there just wasn't any. The Nixon touch-down in China was so low-keyed in fact that NBC's Edwin Newman found himself filling up network time by analysing the Nixon-Chou En-lai handshake.

In the midst of all this news scarcity and confusion, Barbara Walters ultimately was the one American correspondent who came out smelling like a rose. With so little political and diplomatic news to go around, her intensive coverage of Pat Nixon garnered the biggest headlines of the trip to China. Barbara's success in the face of her colleagues' collective disaster, however, did not exactly make her the social hit of the Peking season. American photographers reportedly were so infuriated with Barbara—for standing so close to the First Lady all week that she wound up in nearly every photograph—that in Shanghai they dumped a mountain of ruined film in her hotel room.

Barbara angered her fellow correspondents in other ways, too. They called her snobbish because she didn't say good morning to them, and they found her difficult to work with because she refused to pool her information with them. NBC's John Chancellor, however, feels Barbara may have been a bit scapegoated on the China trip. In his estimation, she worked hard and certainly pulled her own weight. She did so well, in fact, that she cornered more airtime than any other membr of the NBC China news team, and unquestionably, she was a major reason why her own network captured the highest ratings of all three in China coverage.

In her own defense, Barbara felt she was handicapped in her Nixon China assignment, being pitted against the top newsmen in American journalism. It made her feel very inadequate. All her old shyness and inhibitions returned to haunt her.

But whether or not Barbara Walters made any friends or enemies in the press corps during her China jaunt is really beside the point. The plain fact of the matter is that she went to China as the female regular on NBC's *Today* show and came hom a brand-new superstar!

CHAPTER VIII

Friend and Enemy

"If you have a real problem, Barbara Walters will be the first one to help you."
—Stuart Schulberg,
Executive Producer of
the **Today** show.

The people who really know Barbara Walters love her. Larry Johnson, producer of *Not For Women Only*, admits that Barbara occasionally gets carried away with her own viewpoint during a planning conference or a film-editing session. But just a few minutes later, she'll purr in your ear, "I know I've been a cat. I didn't mean it."

Stuart Schulberg, *Today's* executive producer, has even more praise for his female co-host. "If you have a real problem, Barbara will be the first one to help you," Mr. Schulberg maintains, adding that when one of the cast or crew is in serious trouble Barbara invariably locks her office door, accepts no phone calls and goes into a prolonged, heart-to-heart huddle with the friend in need.

Many of Barbara's personal friends are women she met through *Today* show encounters. She corresponds regularly with

Muriel Humphrey, Ann Landers and Coretta King, all of whom she came to know first as morning interview subjects. Another close set of personal friends are Alan King and his wife, who often invite Barbara to dinner parties at their beautiful Long Island home (where the guest list includes film stars as well as senators). Dorothy Rodgers (wife of composer Richard Rodgers) and well-known TV panelists Arlene Francis and Kitty Carlisle also travel in the same social circle as Ms. Walters.

One celebrity whom Barbara almost feuded with before they even met was comedienne Joan Rivers. In a *New York Times* interview, Ms. Rivers, talking about tough and aggressive women, had let fly with "I'd love to put Barbara Walters and Jacqueline Susann in the same room and see which one came out alive." Ironically enough, Barbara had just written Joan Rivers a flattering note welcoming her to NBC as hostess of a new talk show. Joan received Barbara's note just one day before her *Times* interview was slated to roll off the press. She immediately phone Barbara to apologize beforehand and as a result of that conversation the two ladies became chums.

When thirty-two year old Sally Quinn left *The Washington Post* in August 1973 to become anchorwoman of the *CBS Morning*

News opposite Barbara Walters, not everyone hoped they would become chums. In fact, it seemed to work more to the networks' advantage to stir up some sort of colossal cat fight between the girls and thereby generate publicity. Television viewers, of course, have thrived on "celebrity feuds" from way back. They loved it when Jack Paar feuded with Ed Sullivan, and even more so later on, when he went on ABC in late-night competition against *Tonight's* Johnny Carson. A feud between TV's only two reigning breakfast queens promised to be even more delicious. The only problem was that Sally and Barbara refused to play along.

A month before Sally arrived at CBS, Aaron Latham reported in *New York Magazine* that both Sally and Barbara were insisting that their battle for ratings wasn't going to turn into a personal hair-pulling contest ("It is sexist even to imply such a thing," Latham wrote). Indeed, Barbara Walters had just dashed off a letter to Sally Quinn—a brief note, really—with three main points: 1) in Barbara's opinion, CBS couldn't have found themselves a better anchor girl anywhere; 2) she looked forward to socializing with Sally now that they'd both be New Yorkers; and 3) she urged Sally to take a mutual pledge with her to steer clear of all those columnists who would try to build their rather delicate career competition into a feud.

In terms of background and upbringing, Barbara Walters and Sally Quinn were hardly cut out of the same mold, yet there are strange parallels in their past. The daughter of an Army general, Sally was born in Savannah, Georgia, and grew up in a succession of exotic locales—Japan, Greece, Germany, the American Far West—as her father moved from one military base to another. Barbara, the daughter of nightclub producer Lou Walters, also grew up moving from one show town to another. In every new town, Sally had to learn new rules of girlhood survival; so did Barbara. Knowing the right shoes to wear became very important. In the East, Sally learned to wear loafers; in the West, saddle shoes were her passport to social acceptability. Barbara Walters had her teenage foot troubles, too. During her first day at a Manhattan private school, she drew critical attention to herself wearing Cuban heels and bobby socks. She didn't know it was considered a gauche combination.

There were other above-the-ankle similarities, too. Barbara wanted to major in drama at Sarah Lawrence but never did. Sally, who filled out her placement office questionnaire at Smith College by writing that she wanted to be a famous movie star, did major in drama at Smith, and was even spotted by an M-G-M talent scout in a college production of *The Skin of our Teeth*.

Barbara Walters met Sally Quinn in 1971 when Salley did a profile on her for *The Washington Post*. Little did Sally suspect that a year-and-a-half later she would be challenging Barbara as earlybird ratings champ on a competing network. With the *Today* show a twenty-year-old Nielsen winner, taking over the *CBS Morning News* (which debuted in 1965) wasn't perhaps the riskiest job in the world—but damn close! (In an ironic bit of TV history, Barbara Walters had once written for a CBS early-morning entry that failed, starring what had to be the definitive odd couple of the century—Walter Cronkite and Dick Van Dyke.) Before Sally joined the *CBS Morning News*, such veteran newscasters as Mike Wallace, John Hart and Bernard Kalb had already tried and failed to raise CBS' early-morning ratings from a sad half the number of shares that NBC brings in.

When Sally resigned from the *Post* to launch her television career, she confided to a fellow *Post* reporter that when she and Barbara Walters had both covered the Shah of Iran's lavish celebration in 1971 they had shared the same sleeping quarters. Sally implied that rooming as reporters covering the same event was like being in combat together—and that competing against each other on the small screen every day would be a similar situation.

Well, as it all turned out, a real drag-out-knock-down cat fight never did develop between the two girls. But, as it also turned out, Sally Quinn didn't remain on the CBS airwaves long enough to pose a genuine threat to *Today's* Barbara Walters. She retired from television not long ago without having made a sizable dent in the early-morning Nielsens. She wrote up the whole bittersweet experience in a recently issued book called *We're Going to Make You a Star*.

If Barbara Walters was able to adroitly navigate her way through the Sally Quinn affair, she has done an even more artful job avoiding combat with her own male co-stars. Over the years, she has shared the *Today* spotlight with a succession of top newscasters; and while Barbara has never stood in anyone's shadow as a TV personality, she has recognized the fact that she is only *one half* of a very good team and acted accordingly.

Barbara's first anchorman was Hugh Downs, whom she calls one of the most charming men she has ever know. In *How to Talk with Practically Anybody about Practically Anything*, Barbara relates that Hugh was so gentlemanly and polite as *Today* host that the crew had only one way of guessing that he might be upset or impatient with a guest—if he called the guest "sir" too much.

Without a question, Downs' trademark has always been his easygoing style. The son of a Lima, Ohio tire and battery dealer, he attended Bluffton College and Wayne State University, but never actually received a degree. He picked up most of his higher education by self-study, and did such a fine job of making himself knowledgeable on a wide range of subjects that, during his tenure as Jack Paar's straight man, he became known as the *Tonight* show's resident intellectual. Hugh Downs had a penchant for explaining things and Jack Paar was forever ribbing him about it on the air. Once, Paar was telling the audience how he'd almost tipped over while on water skis. That let Downs into a two minute lecture on the mechanics of water-skiing, until Paar finally quipped: "Hugh, when you drown, at least you'll know the reason why!"

Downs had gotten his broadcasting start at the age of 19, first as program director of

WLOK, the Lima radio station, then as an announcer for Detroit's WWJ. His Army career during World War II lasted exactly four weeks. He collapsed in the middle of basic training and earned a medical discharge. When television came along, Hugh worked as announcer for the *Kukla, Fran and Ollie* show, then did the same chores for Arlene Francis in her New York based *Home* program. He went to work for Jack Paar in 1957—when he was already host of the popular daytime game show, *Concentration*—and by 1960 his combined NVC income was $140,000 a year.

In 1962, after five years with the *Tonight* show, Hugh Downs became *Today's* host. He was chosen for the spot over a number of other top newscasters because of his basic middle-of-the-road, all-American appeal to women (*Today's* viewership consists of far more women than men). Shelley Winters had once called him "a method announcer." According to *Time Magazine*, a TV critic once summed up the secret of Downs' success as follows: "He looks like everybody's son-in-law, very sincere and stunningly good at nothing." Downs became so famous for his relaxed manner and complete unflappability that an NBC cameraman once said: "This guy makes Perry Como look like a nervous wreck."

As host of the *Today* show, although he could not sing, dance, juggle or tell jokes, Hugh Downs drew the highest salary on the NBC payroll. Part of the reason why he drew that salary was because Downs supposedly occupied the hottest seat in television. Doing a live, two-hour morning news and talk show was anxiety-producing. The battle for ratings was equally anxiety-producing. But Hugh Downs never let one feather get ruffled. If all the scenery had ever collapsed around him as the studio slowly burned to the ground, he probably would have casually done the last commercial—then rushed for the fire exit!

"The moment you begin worrying about details," Hugh told *Saturday Evening Post* writer Peter Maas in November 1962, "you become a candidate for a psychiatric ward! I was never a scrambler, but I used to push harder than I do now. Then I formulated the idea not to take everything so seriously. In this business everything is urgent. When I get a memo marked 'urgent,' I put it under my desk. I find a couple of weeks later that it isn't so urgent anymore."

Married since 1944 to the former Ruth Shaheen and the father of two—a son, Hugh Raymond, and a daughter, Deirdre Linda—Hugh Downs was the epitome of the classic family man. Just how much wholesomeness was an inherent part of his image was revealed one time when Downs and Jack Paar were discussing marital strife on the *Tonight* show. Without thinking, Downs mentioned that during his own first year of marriage, Ruth and he had battled a lot—in fact he even once belted her! The public outcry was incredible. "I've never gotten so much mail in my life. Belting your wife in this country is apparently worse than being a Communist!" Downs told Peter Maas.

During their seven years as *Today's* team, Barbara Walters and Hugh Downs enjoyed a warm, friendly relationship. It's a friendship that's continued right up to the present. This fall Downs has joined Ms. Walters as alternate host of *Not For Women Only*—his first regular national TV role since bowing out of the *Today* show "to move to other interests" in October 1971. The current plan of action calls for Downs to moderate eighteen weeks' worth of shows and Barbara Walters to moderate the other eighteen weeks. (Splitting the hosting chores with Hugh Downs has allowed Barbara time to handle other TV chores. This summer she flew to Europe to interview several reigning and deposed monarchs for an NBC daytime special, *The Royal Lovers*; and from now until July 4,

1976 she and Jim Hartz are traveling to every state of the Union commemorating Bicentennial Year on the *Today* show.)

Following Down's departure in 1971, the *Today* helm was taken over by Frank McGee, who stayed with the show until his death in 1974. McGee was actually the fourth man to moderate the program. Aside from Downs, Dave Garroway and John Chancellor had also held the reins. Born on September 12, 1921 in Monroe, Louisiana, Frank was raised among the oil derricks of Oklahoma and Louisiana, where his stepfather worked on a drilling crew. Oil excavating is a rootless, unpredictable way of life. Like Barbara Walters, as a child Frank McGee never lived in one place for very long. "As a kid, I lived in more towns than I can remember," he often said. "Some don't even exist today."

Determined not to spend the rest of his life in the oil fields, Frank set out for greener pastures right after high school. He attended both the University of Oklahoma and the University of California, although he had no high school diploma. He had failed to graduate from Norman, Oklahoma high school because he refused to apologize to a teacher with whom he had argued. The teacher had been unfairly riding herd on one of Frank's classmates. Frank chose to defend the boy—and she flunked him. It was his first lesson in the price of idealism but it didn't temper his idealism any.

In fact, that was how Frank McGee earned a reputation for himself as a news broadcaster. After starting off as a radio announcer on WKY in Oklahoma City, he rose to national prominence in the 1950s covering the historic civil rights movement emerging in Montgomery, Alabama. Frank became the first radio or TV journalist to interview Martin Luther King. During the 1960s, he covered the Apollo space flights and Presidential conventions before becoming anchorman of the *NBC Nightly News*. Like Hugh Downs, Frank McGee was also a family man. Married in 1942, he and his wife Susan made their home in Scarsdale, New York. They were the parents of a son, Michael, and a daughter, Sharon.

Following Frank's death in April 1974, it was a toss-up as to who would become *Today's* fifth anchorman. Among the frequently mentioned candidates were Garrick Utley (who filled in on an interim basis), Tom Snyder and Edwin Newman. Eventually, though, the job went to Jim Hartz, anchorman of NBC's *News Center 4*. At the same time, after ten years on the air, Barbara Walters was finally elevated to co-host rank on the *Today* show and the network promised to create four specials for her.

Like his predecessor, Jim Hartz is a native Oklahoman. Born on February 3, 1940—which makes him nine years younger than Barbara, the first anchorman who is actually her junior—Jim grew up in Tulsa, Oklahoma. As a pre-medical student at the University of Tulsa, he worked as a reporter for a local radio station, WRMG. In 1962, he decided to leave his medical studies for a career as a newsman and joined KOTV in Tulsa. Two years later, on April 13, 1964, he moved to NBC News, New York where he stayed until July 29, 1974, his first day on the *Today* show.

Until *Today* called, Jim, his wife Nor and their three children—Jana, John and Nancy—lived out on Long Island. But the early morning commute to NBC's Studio 3K, where the *Today* show emanates, proved too much. "I found myself having to leave home by 4 a.m." Jim said recently. "Even though a chauffeured car picked me up, I'd be thoroughly exhausted before we even reached Manhattan." So, after several weeks of this crazy, fatiguing regimen, Jim and Norma set out to find a new home. They wound up with an elegant townhouse right in midtown Manhattan. "At the moment, we're still trying to furnish it," Jim says. "I spend Saturdays and every free weekday afternoon I have scouring Manhattan with Norma for a dining-room set and living room furniture." But although Jim is willing to contribute his decorating ideas when it comes to home furnishing, he refuses to shop for his own clothes. "I let Norma run the show when it comes to picking out my clothes," he admits. "I'm tasteless in that department."

Like every celebrity who has ever monitored the *Today* desk, Jim Hartz doesn't love the working hours. Because he has to get up at such an ungodly hour every morning, he and Norma rarely go out socially, or even entertain much at home. For relaxation, he goes bike-riding with his kids in Central Park or takes his wife out to dinner on the weekend or limbers up on the NBC softball team. He doesn't catch much evening TV because he's usually in bed and fast asleep by 10 p.m. on week nights. "However, there are those rare nights," he concedes, "when I get hooked on a movie and stay up far too late for my own good."

Although Jim has been with NBC practically his entire working life, his role has been far from sedentary. His assignments have included covering the lunar landings, the dedication of the Lyndon Baines Johnson Library and the outbreak of the Arab-

Israeli War in October 1973. Reporting first hand on the shelling action on the Golan Heights, at one point Jim and the whole NBC camera crew were forced to stop filming and take cover when their jeep became a moving target in the crossfire.

Co-hosting the *Today* show is certainly a lot less dangerous, although Jim had only one complaint about his new assignment. He thinks it's awkward and unrealistic to expect performers who appear on the program to be at their shining best at 7 a.m. As proof of his argument, he cites the day Lionel Hampton was a *Today* guest and Jim mentioned to the famed jazz musician that he thought he looked tired. "I sure am, man," Lionel replied. "I haven't been to bed yet. I was up all night and here at 4 a.m. to pre-rehearse."

Still, Jim Hartz and Barbara Walters must be doing something right. Barbara won an Emmy as "best daytime talk host"— and even though Jim was nominated in the same category and lost, in her acceptance speech Barbara noted that she felt half the award was rightfully his. That was in May. A month later, on June 25, 1975, both Jim and Barbara tied in the Afternoon TV Magazine Writers and Editors Awards competition as this year's "best talk hosts." (*Today* won as "best talk show" as well). The awards were presented in the Promenade Cafe at Rockefeller Center, only seven floors down from Jim, and Barbara's office doorstep. In the Afternoon TV competition, their tie represented a triumph over a tough field of nominees that included Mike Douglas, Bill Beutel and Pat Collins.

For Barbara Walters, it was just one more blitz in an eleven-year winning streak.

CHAPTER IX

"Hattie Conners"

"Hattie . . . If Hugh Hefner wanted you to pose in the nude with Jackie Kennedy, Maria Callas, the Queen of England, Felicia Bernstein, Mama Cass, and Pat Nixon, would you? . . . ."
". . . Have the others agreed to do it?"
—excerpt from **The Whole World is Watching**, a 1972 novel by ex-**Today** producer Al Morgan

In 1972, Al Morgan, the man who produced the *Today* show for nine years and is generally credited with "discovering" Barbara Walters, published a novel called *The Whole World is Watching*. The setting of the novel is the 1968 Democratic Presidential Convention in Chicago and the violence that erupted between Mayor Daley's police and the student demonstrators who poured into the city.

The sickening, unparalleled events that took place during those August dog days in Chicago are seen through the eyes of a network news team covering the convention, namely, the producer, crew and stars of the *Now* show, an early-morning talk fest that obviously resembles the *Today* show.

In his prologue to the novel, Morgan makes the specific point that the story that follows is *not* about the *Today* program and that the novel's narrator is not a thinly veiled replica of the author. Furthermore, the book's other main characters are not modeled after Hugh Downs, Barbara Walters and Joe Garagiola. They are all "composites"—although Morgan hopes the reader will find them believable and compelling.

The story unfolds through the eyes and ears of Gary Sutton, thirty-nine years-old producer of the *Now* show who possesses an abundance of negative and positive attributes. On the negative side, he drinks too much, has a temper that's too quick for his own good (for example, he goads his limousine driver, a moonlighting Chicago cop, in the middle of a traffic jam) and he occasionally plays practical jokes on his inept, rather Ted Baxterish anchorman (he once sent him a fake plaque from a fake organization commending him on his use of cliches). On the positive side, Gary Sutton is loyal to his girlfriend (the *Now* press representative) and even a bit of a hero when history demands it (his blood-and-guts coverage of the convention riots—showing college kids being clubbed and maced by the Chicago police—eventually costs him his job).

The stars of the *Now* show are all unique in their own right. Newt Johns, the *Now* anchorman, is a boob who somehow manages to make his off-screen dullness come across on-screen as an air of mild-mannered erudition. Pete Martinez, *Now's* second banana, is a former boxing champ with a blue-collar outlook who is pro-cop and anti-student until he accidentally gets mauled by one of Daley's blue knights. But by far and away the most intriguing member of the *Now* team is female regular Hattie Conners, whom the back cover of the paperback edition describes as "the fabulous woman interviewer whose beauty and brains made her a homescreen superstar."

While the other characters in the book get clubbed in Lincoln Park, fired in a network purge, or at least smashing drunk at middle-of-the-night press parties, Hattie simply goes about her business of trying to find the best hairdresser in Chicago and the right outfit to wear to convention hall. Along the way, she also managed to land prize interviews with a couple of candidates' wives and tape a mind-blowing feature segment with a student protester from Swarthmore College who has brought along his wife and their infant to the Chicago sit-ins.

Hattie Conners is not Barbara Walters, by any means—but there are strange parallels. Hattie is constantly worried about her hair, her clothes, and her standing with the beautiful people. Barbara Walters worries about her hair, her clothes, and spends a good many evenings in the company of New York's beautiful people. When Barbara first became a *Today* regular, she was occasionally criticized for a so-called "aggressive" approach. Early in Al Morgan's novel, Hattie moans to Gary Sutton that she knows she interrupts Newt Johns too much on the air—the trouble is she just can't help it. Too many times Newt hasn't bothered to read the book or see the movie he's supposed to be talking about but she has. So, feeling she owes it to the guest, she just naturally jumps in and kind of hogs the interview.

Later on in the book, producer and anchor girl get into a heated discussion about the social merits of Hugh Hefner's *Playboy Magazine*. Gary Sutton maintains that *Playboy* has tremendous social value—it lets frustrated men vent their sexual urges without becoming rapists in the process. Hattie Connors thinks it's a sexist publication that degrades and exploits women (anyway, she knows it can't be a worthwhile magazine. She's never seen a copy on the Leonard Bernsteins' coffee table).

So, Gary Sutton poses a philosophical dilemma:

"Hattie. . . . If Hugh Hefner wanted you

to pose in the nude with Jackie Kennedy, Maria Callas, the Queen of England, Felicia Bernstein, Mama Cas, and Pat Nixon, would you?"

Hattie asks how Mama Cass—certainly not the *Playboy* ideal—wound up on the list.

Gary doesn't answer that one; but he tells her that by posing nude with these celebrities, she quite possibly may end the Vietnam war, cure cancer and save starving Indian children, among other things.

Hattie asks, "Have the others agreed to do it?"

"For cancer, Vietnam peace and starving children?"

"Then, in that case, of course I would."

"Fine. I was just trying to find out your price."

At another point in the book, one of the characters lambastes all the *Now* stars as being glossy robots, with no backbone or conviction. He suggests that if Americans ever passed a referendum condoning the broiling of babies, Hattie would nonchalantly attend the roast, clucking over what to wear and whether a limousine would be at her service.

Hilty Reardon, Gary Sutton's press-department girlfriend, snaps back in Hattie's defense. "That's not fair," she said.

"She's good. She's new at being a celebrity, and she overprotects her status because she can't believe it's going to last."

That may be the best explanation of Barbara Walters, or any woman in the male-dominated network news field today.

Nevertheless, although *some* of the Barbara Walters Al Morgan has known and worked with may have gone into the minting of Hattie Conners, they remain two entirely different women. There are, in fact, great differences between them. For one thing, Hattie is single—totally devoted to her job, a glamorous workhorse outfitted by Bergdorf Goodman and educated by *Saturday Review*. Barbara Walters is not single. For nine years (her first eight years on the *Today* show) she was a very married lady; and even these days her daughter Jacqueline certainly receives as much of her energy and attention as her TV duties. And Barbara Walters, an author in her own right who has written one best-seller and contributed numerous pieces to *Ladies Home Journal* and other national magazines over the years, could hardly be called superficial in her taste, outlook or beliefs. She is a *worldly* woman in the true sense of the word who, certainly, from time to time, may find herself seated at a dinner party brushing shoulders with Leonard Bernstein

—but chances are she would find Lawrence Welk charming, too. She is not striving to be "in." She simply respects talent, charm and graciousness wherever she encounters it.

There is also the problem of Hattie Conners' social life (or lack of it), another vast difference between her and Barbara Walters. In one chapter of *The Whole World is Watching*, shortly after the crew's arrival in Chicago, Hattie phones Gary Sutton and makes a bit of a fool of herself trying to entice him to take her out to dinner. The scene reads like something out of *Miss Lonelyhearts*: she's the glamorous TV star with a suitcase full of beautiful dresses and no one to wear them for; out of desperation, she calls her producer, unaware that she's caught him in bed curled up with his girl friend. Now that doesn't sound at all like Barbara Walters. True, at the moment, she may be *sans* husband, but she's never at a loss for escorts. Since her parting of the ways with Lee Guber, she may even have become seriously involved with someone else. "I wouldn't be the least surprised," says one Walters intimate, "if Barbara eventually married for a third time. Deep down, I think she's really the kind of woman who likes to be married."

Still, Hattie Conners lives on. In Al Morgan's next book, a 1974 release called *Anchorwoman*, Hattie goes even farther than Barbara Walters ever dreamed possible. She leaves the *Now* show to become the network's first primetime anchorwoman (something none of the big three networks have yet tried in real life) and joins the ranks of an elite video club that includes Walter Cronkite, John Chancellor and Eric Sevareid. Enroute to her new position, however, Hattie is sent to cover a presidential visit to the Virgin Islands. In the midst of a very ordinary assignment, she lands the most explosive story of her career. To reveal it threatens the security of the White House. Not to reveal it jeopardizes her job as a credible TV correspondent. It's a dilemma that makes for fast-paced, exciting reading.

Unlike *The Whole World is Watching*, where Hattie Conners was simply a supporting character, *Anchorwoman* is her very own book and she emerges an attractive and moving contemporary heroine.

The novel opens, in true Barbara Walters fashion, with Hattie Conners' alarm clock going off at 4:15 a.m. What follows is Hattie's instinctive, pre-coffee and warm shower reaction to that dehumanizing fact of life. "No matter how large the salary checks got, no matter how soft the back seat in the limo, no matter how many cover stories, signed authgraphs, or free vacations in the Greek islands, she never got used to that. Four-fifteen!" It may be the best commentary on the lifestyle of the *Today* people ever written. He describes Hattie's wake-up ritual with military precision: after a warm shower, she slips into slacks and shirt carefully laid out the night before; then, over a steaming cup of black instant coffee, she listens to the 4:30 a.m. news at her kitchen table. Five minutes later, she rides the elevator down to a waiting limousine, and on the way to the studio waves to an all-night newsstand operator on Fiftieth Street. Whether or not Barbara Walters waves to any West Side news dealers on her way to work is questionable. Otherwise, the routine sounds strangely familiar.

While Hattie settles down to have breakfast in her dressing room two hours before airtime, the reader learns two interesting things about her working life. First, there is a month-by-month schedule of the dresses she'll wear on the show, hanging in the producer's office. Hattie doesn't choose her own outfits because the choice of how she'll look to fifteen million viewers, a good percentage of them women in nightgowns, is too important to be left *merely* to her. Secondly, Hattie has her own bathroom next to her dressing room. She is one of the few stars who does. It gives her more clout than her salary or her face on the cover of *Time Magazine*, and was a major bone of contention in her last contract. Installing a private powder room for her was one of the most expensive concessions the network could make since pipes had to be brought in from a distance of five hundred feet. The bathroom is Hattie's exclusive property— even visiting dignitaries she interviews wouldn't dream of using it.

But somehow or other, it always comes back to a matter of sleep lost, or rather sleep irretrievably lost. When Hattie first learns that her *Now* days are over, and a new life is about to open up for her as an evening anchorwoman, it isn't the status or challenge of the job that thrills her. It's the hours. She bubbles to her secretary that from now on she'll be able to sleep till seven-thirty in the morning and stay up till midnight if she wants to. She can even order wine with dinner and not dread a hangover the next morning!

No, Hattie Conners isn't Barbara Walters, not by a longshot. But if Barbara ever suddenly found herself anchoring the *NBC Nightly News*, chances are her reaction would be just as predictable—a great, big joyful yawn that she's been holding back bravely for eleven years now!

CHAPTER X

Today's Woman

"I'm not beautiful, slick or glamorous . . . anybody can be like me."
—Barbara Walters talking to Sally Quinn.

Barbara Walters thinks she knows the reason for her enormous success. "I'm not beautiful, slick or glamorous," she once confided in a *Washington Post* interview written by Sally Quinn. "I may be one of the most envied women in America. And only because anybody can be like me. They can't be Carol Burnett if they can't sing; they can't be a great dancer if they can't dance; they can't be a great actress if they can't act. They can be like me."

But Barbara Walters is wrong. Although she thinks she appeals to the housewives of America because she doesn't look like she just stepped out of a movie screen or the cover of *Vogue*, her image certainly isn't as ordinary and lackluster as she pretends. What the women of America see when they wake up to Barbara Walters every morning is someone who is sophisticated, clever, articulate and one hundred percent feminine.

She is neither a cuddly beauty nor a well-programmed robot. Mainly, what she projects is charm and intelligence—two qualities that American women seem to prize very highly.

All in all, Barbara's TV image is far from middle-of-the-road or middle-American. She is what she is—an educated cosmopolitan—not a model homemaker like Betty White; not the wise-cracking bridge club lady like Virginia Graham. Yet Barbara Walters fits very well into the American scheme of things. Perhaps that has to do with the clever way she's been packaged and presented on the *Today* show.

To offset her intellectual, Eastern Establishment image, Barbara has consistently been paired with anchormen who are all solid, midwestern *Father Knows Best* types. Hugh Downs came from Lima, Ohio; both Frank McGee and Jim Hartz grew up in Oklahoma. All three are fairhaired, churchgoing types—good husbands and model fathers. This combination of the fairhaired football player and the exotic culture *maven* seems to hold a great deal of enchantment for Americans. It's partly the classic male-female battle of wits waged in movie after movie by Spencer Tracy and Katharine Hepburn. It's the Camelot legend, exemplified by all-American PT-109 commander John F. Kennedy and his ballet-loving French-speaking wife, Jacqueline. It's the bittersweet love story of the Jewish girl and the WASP—Barbra Streisand and Robert Redford in *The Way We Were.*

Perhaps Barbara Walters also appeals to millions of women because she herself is *a woman of our times.* She is liberated without being a crusader; an aggressive career gal who still gets doors opened and cabs hailed for her. And she wouldn't want it any other way. Barbara represents the subdued, non-bra-burning middle path of feminism. In her own life, she has sought a career, competed with men in TV news departments (a highly male-dominated area) and gone much farther than any *Today* girl before her. Yet, she has not abandoned the traditional feminine role in the process. She still worries about her hair, frames her six-year-old daughter's report cards and engages heavily in the rather old-fashioned ritual of "dating."

Feminist writer Gloria Steinem considers Barbara Walters "a transitional person" in the field of television. Gloria told *The New York Times Magazine* that "in an earlier state of consciousness (pre-Women's Lib era), she was one of the few women on television not just serving coffee. She asks the same questions as a male interviewer, but women realize that she's sympathetic." According to Ms. Steinem, Barbara has to ask what she calls "male" questions because "the adult world still has male values." So, in a very real sense, Barbara Walters is a buffer bridging the two opposing female camps in America today—the ladies in the kitchen and the girls in the consciousness-raising groups.

That same *N.Y. Times Magazine* article brought Ms. Walters' personal views on the women's lib movement into even sharper perspective by revealing her thoughts on legalized abortion. Privately, Barbara is all for it; but she refused to sign a *Ms. Magazine* petition saying that she'd had one herself. Aside from the fact that Barbara Walters has never had an abortion, she feels her image as an objective reporter prevents her from taking a public stand. Furthermore, despite all the social change they've initiated, Barbara thinks "militant feminists have . . . given American women a kind of national inferiority complex." There's something unappealing, says Barbara, about women who wage verbal wars on television.

Whether you feel Barbara is too liberated or not liberated enough, there's no denying that at present she is the most important woman on the daytime television scene. On her own network, NBC, the only females who have been holding court (during daylight hours) as long as Barbara are two serial queens—Jacqueline Courtney of *Another World* and Elizabeth Hubbard of *The Doctors*. Aside from Barbara, by far the most intriguing woman at Rockefeller Center is Lin Bolen, the young network vice-president in charge of daytime programming (Lin holds the distinction of being the first female ever to hold that title). Lin took over the NBC daytime reins two years ago after developing several series for primetime television, including the popular Rock Hudson-Susan St. James mystery show, *McMillan and Wife*. At 30 Rockefeller Center, Lin has devoted herself primarily to developing new game shows and serials. Her highly touted new-wave soap opera, *How to Survive a Marriage* didn't survive the ratings, but her idea of expanding both *Another World* and *Days of our Lives* into hour-long shows has. Occasionally, though, Lin Bolen and Barbara Walters do cross paths. In May 1974, when NBC hosted the first daytime Emmy award presentations at Rockefeller Center, Lin enlisted Barbara Walters to serve as co-host for the occasion. She was teamed with *Hollywood Squares'* Peter Marshall. Barbara's familiarity with the vagaries of live broadcasting came in handy when the award presentations unexpectedly finished earlier than anyone had calculated. Ms. Walters and Mr. Marshall were left holding the bag with several minutes of empty airtime. Barbara rished in and adroitly filled the vacuum by taking a quick tour of the Rockefeller Center audience with her trusty hand microphone. She did instant interviews with Dinah Shore (who'd just learned that even an Emmy couldn't keep her from being cancelled by NBC; her daytime variety show was later picked up by CBS) and Irene Powell (who, at that time, was headlining on Broadway in *Irene*).

Barbara's TV chores may seem childishly easy to the casual viewer ("What does she do that any average housewife couldn't do?" dissident fans often inquire), but there's far more to being a successful talk host than meets the eye—or ear. The list of female casualties on the daytime talk-show circuit is staggering: Joan Rivers, Helen Gurley Brown, Pat Collins, Sally Quinn, Betsy Palmer, Betty White and scores of others have all tried their hand at making TV small talk on a variety of subjects and either failed outright or met with only limited success. True, Virginia Graham's *Girl Talk* was a popular entry for several years (until she left the show in a contract dispute) and Dinah Shore's *Dinah!* is now enjoying a healthy run on CBS, despite its cancellation by NBC. But those are the exceptions.

The achievement record of women on the nighttime talkshow scene is even more dismal. One of the foremost disasters was *The Joyce and Barbara Show*—pairing Joyce Susskind and Barbara Howar—on New York's WNEW in 1970. According to Ms. Howar's account of the fiasco in her autobiographical best-seller *Laughing All The Way*, the idea of teaming two ladies on a syndicated nighttime talk show was originally conceived by Metromedia executive Robert Bennett. The two ladies he had in mind were Barbara Howar and Gloria Steinem, and the intention was to prove that women on nighttime television could draw ratings without singing, dancing, being funny or selling laundry bleach. When Metromedia had to drop out of the project because of financial troubles, David Susskind came to the rescue. At that point, Gloria Steinem walked out and David's wife, Joyce, walked in. From the start, the show did not go well on-screen or off. Barbara and David Susskind fought. Barbara and Joyce Susskind fought. It turned out to be one of the briefest experiments ever tried on nighttime television.

In recent years, there has been a great deal of conjecture that Barbara Walters may be contemplating taking the big plunge into the primetime arena. But the outlook is doubtful. "Why should NBC move Barbara out of her *Today* slot, where she's virtually unchallengeable, and risk both the show's success and her own by giving her a news anchor spot or a talk show at night?"

Who, in the final analysis, is the *real* Barbara Walters—the woman behind the myth, the flesh-and-blood figure behind the glossy TV image?

Barbara herself doesn't delve deeply into astrology, but the stars, for all her refusal to gaze meditatively at them, do reveal a great deal about her nature. Born September 25, Barbara's sun sign, guiding her personality, is Libra, the seventh sign of the zodiac, ruled by the planet Venus, best described by the key words *harmony* and *partnership*.

As a Libran, Barbara's penchant for partnership, especially where her working life is concerned, should be obvious. The sphere she chose to make her mark in was as co-host of the *Today* show. She has always worked well on television with a male partner, and has maintained unwavering friendly relationships with all her gentlemen teammates.

Partnership in the romantic sphere is also a trademark of Librans. They tend to marry young (Barbara's first ill-fated marriage occurred shortly after college graduation); and, if the marriage doesn't work out, they generally don't become shy of the institution itself. As far as emotional relationships go, "falling in love with love" is par for the course for those ruled by affection-craving Venus. Librans need romance the way Capricorns lust after status or Scorpios demand power. When in love, they like to be wooed with soft music and thoughtful gestures. The male in love becomes chivalrous; the female in love melts like butter. Burt Bachrach's hit tune "What the World Needs Now is Love, Sweet Love" must have been written with a Libran in mind.

Is it really any wonder, then, why one of the first things Barbara Walters wanted to know when she arrived in China was whether romantic love is still flourishing under the Communist regime? "Do people marry for love?" she asked a rather straight-laced interpreter. "No," he replied. Barbara was obviously disappointed by his answer. Yet, the real China may not be all that it appears to be on the surface—for this ancient nation is ruled by Libra, too.

(Yes, nations also have sun signs, astrologically speaking. The U.S. is under Geminian influence; England is ruled by Taurus.) Considering this fact it shouldn't have shocked or surprised Barbara very much to discover a line of aphrodisiacs on sale in a Peking pharmacy. After all, with no romantic novels to read or weepy movies to see, that Libran romanticism just has to surface somewhere!

Positively speaking, Librans are noted for their charm and diplomacy (two qualities which Barbara obviously prizes in her interview subjects and social escorts). They require pleasant living conditions (Barbara's West Side Manhattan apartment is full of bright, sunny colors and comfortable furniture. Her remark to *House Beautiful* was "there's no place in the living room where you can't put your feet up.") Harmony is equally important to her nature. Barbara Walters wouldn't dream of being seen publicly dressed in anything less than impeccable taste, and the need for harmony rules her personal relationships as well.

Seeking harmony in life, the Libran will tend to avoid quarrels and open confrontations at all costs. Celebrated Libran, Eleanor Roosevelt, rarely fought with anyone—including her husband. The lengths she went to in order to avert conflict reportedly included allowing FDR's mistress, Missy LeHand, to live in the New York governor's mansion, under the family roof. In her own attempt to keep harmony at all costs in her life, Barbara Walters may have been willing to settle for supporting-player status on the *Today* show for so long simply because she loathed an open battle with NBC. Possibly, her refusal to fight for co-host recognition is what kept the title out of her reach till recently.

What does the future hold for Barbara Walters? First and foremost, there is a seemingly endless future assured her at her trusty, old *Today* desk. In a little more than a decade, Barbara may have interviewed a hefty share of world leaders, movie stars, artists, social crusaders and fanatics of all shapes and sizes, but she hadn't licked the pot clean by any means. There are still a great many superheroes of one sort or another who haven't traded TV small talk with Barbara Walters. Although Barbara has interviewed England's Prince Philip and covered Prince Charles' investiture first-hand, she has never managed to lure Queen Elizabeth herself before the magic cameras. Nor has she ever interviewed Pope Paul VI, Howard Hughes, Greta Garbo, Christina Onassis, President Amin of Uganda or Prime Minister Indira Gandhi of India. It would be fascinating to watch Barbara try to capture the essence of Alice Cooper on camera or attempt a dialogue with Fidel Castro. Even more fascinating perhaps, considering her closeness to Pat and Dick during the height of the Nixon years, would be the result if Barbara could gain access to San Clemente now and return with a videotape exclusive on Nixon today.

And if her television chores still leave her with an excess of creative energy, Barbara can always return to the typewriter. Her memoirs would be worth a fortune. So would a book on her political prognostications. This woman who has sat inches away from so many revered heads of state, confronted so many diplomats, grilled so many legislators is probably more turned in to the real political state of things than an awful lot of public officials.

Politics, in fact, seems to loom up formidably in any assessment of Barbara Walters' future. Although Barbara herself has never voiced any plans to enter the political arena or seek a diplomatic post, neither option would be a particularly fanciful role for her. Her years as TV's grand inquisitor have certainly taught her a lot in dealing with top-echelon political figures, both foreign and American. Any woman who could charm both Dean Rusk and Spiro Agnew, and find just the right greeting for a Persian shah and an Israeli premier, could certainly hold her own as a full-time politician.

And what a dandy political candidate Barbara Walters might make. After all, what with Shirley Temple serving as U.S. Ambassador to Ghana and Bess Myerson campaigning for a Democratic senatorial nomination in New York, is the idea really so farfetched? Of course, Barbara might have to wait a few years before seeking appointment to the diplomatic corps—at least until there's a turnover in Presidential administrations. You see, despite her non-partisan image as a TV newscaster, Barbara Walters classifies herself in the voting booth as a liberal Democrat. Ironically, the girl who was once labeled "the Nixon pet" by other White House correspondents disagreed strongly with many policies of the Nixon Administration.

Back in the early '70s, when Barbara was busy setting up camera and sound equipment in the White House Blue Room, she herself was in favor of immediate U.S. military withdrawal from Vietnam. She didn't think that Nixon was making much of a positive dent in domestic matters. She was angered by the fact that he disregarded the recommendations of his own commission on population. All in all, Barbara felt Americans had no real idea just how conservative Nixon was in his approach to most issues.

In the political realm, Barbara would definitely be at her best in a strictly diplomatic situation—in fact, the more diplomatic the better. A job like Ambassador to the United Nations would be right up her alley. Or a presidential troubleshooter in the field of education. Few people realize that her favorite subject in the world isn't politics or show business or what the beautiful people are doing. It's children—her own child and everybody else's Barbara's knowledge of the problems affecting children today cuts across all kinds of subdivisions—she knows about mental retardation; she has visited day-care centers in China; she has interviewed the offspring of the rich and famous; she understands firsthand the problems of being a mother who spends more than half her day away from home.

Is Barbara Walters happy with her life? Probably as happy as she'll ever be. She has wealth, power, fame—all the magic things that a little girl backstage in a Miami nightclub once dreamed about. True, she is occasionally lonely, and very often tired, but Barbara is firm believer in the old adage that "nothing comes without great sacrifice." Exactly where she's heading to Barbara herself isn't always quite sure; but ten million faithful *Today* viewers have no worry in that department. They can sleep tight, knowing that just as the sun will rise tomorrow, at 7 a.m. sharp, one second after the NBC peacock flaunts his plumage, a familiar voice will intone: "Good morning . . . I'm Barbara Walters . . . and this is the *Today* show. . . ."

Ten million Americans believe there will always be a Barbara Walters.

And they're right. There will!